Praise for ELEARNING GOLD

Elearning taken to a new level! *Elearning Gold* prepares education administrators for the successful planning and implementing of an exemplary elearning program. Annette Leveque's humorous writing style and utilization of personal experience highlight key concerns and present an unparalleled learning opportunity for the reader.

—*Rhonda Kublin, J.D., M.Ed.*,
Teacher Leader Certification, 15 years teaching
in New York State Middle School.

Annette skillfully detangles human, technical, organizational, strategic, and ethical leadership considerations to make it easy for you to plan, structure, and implement your program. The examples, checklists, and leadership questions make it much easier for both you and your learners. Using this guide is like having a friend and education expert consultant by your side.

—*Cathy Lewis*,
Co-Founder of iSisters Technology Mentoring, Board
Director, University Professor, and Consultant.

This book provides the knowledge and illustrative detail that can become a guide for you in implementing a successful elearning program regardless of where you may be in the world.

—*Govindh Jayaraman,*
Head Coach and Team Lead, IMBA Online Corporation, Author of bestseller Paper Napkin Wisdom: Your Five Step Plan for Life and Business Success

The book centers on the learner experience and simultaneously provides education leaders with a practical approach for designing an online learning world with practical steps to be considered, explored, and addressed. Levesque explains why something matters, includes well-placed personal anecdotes, and offers reflective leadership questions. Whether you're new or experienced in the world of virtual learning and education, Elearning Gold will help you make a difference in the online world.

—*Judy Bauer Puritt, Ph.D.*
in Education (Blended Learning), Business Communications Professor at Algonquin College

Our Malaysian educators quickly adopted Levesque's elearning concepts to help cope with the pandemic and the blended system was quickly accepted by both students and educators. The author provided instructions on how management could review and analyze SWOT, encouraging the use of SMART elearning project goals to explore activities needed to achieve their goals. This book is an asset to managers at all levels.

—*Carl C. Boodram B.A., M.B.A., B.Ed, O.C.T.*

Elearning Gold is a comprehensive manual for the strategic development, coordination, and implementation of a robust virtual education initiative. Levesque provides the clarity and organization necessary to navigate the intricacies of a comprehensive virtual education program that caters to the interests of all key stakeholders: administrators, educators, and students.

—*Nicole M Bulos Barceló, BSc.,*
Licenciatura en Psicologia Clinica,
Middle School Teacher, Cap Cana Heritage School

ELEARNING GOLD

Copyright © 2023 by Annette Levesque.
All rights reserved.
Published by The Canadian Education Station, Ontario, Canada.

ISBN 978-1-7390128-4-7 (hardcover)
ISBN 978-1-7390128-0-9 (paperback)
ISBN 978-1-7390128-1-6 (ebook)

Education / Distance, Open & Online Education
Education / Leadership
Education / Distance

No part of this book may be reproduced or transmitted in any form or by any means, electronic or mechanical, including but not limited to artificial intelligence, photocopying or recording, or by any information storage and retrieval system now known or to be invented or otherwise, without permission in writing from the publisher, except by a reviewer who wishes to quote brief passages in connection with a review written for inclusion in a magazine, newspaper or broadcast.

Please send requests for permission to make copies of any part of this work through the contact form available on the following website:
www.elearninggold.com

The Canadian Education Station
1769 St Laurent Blvd.
Suite 279
Ottawa, ON K1G 3V4
CANADA

The contents of this book are intended to provide the reader with accurate and authoritative information on the subject matter covered. The author and publisher have made every effort to ensure the accuracy of the information herein. The advice and strategies contained herein may not be suitable for every situation. In no event shall the publisher and author be liable for any damages arising out of or in connection with any use of this work, including, but not limited to, any special, incidental, consequential, or other damages. If legal, financial, or other expert assistance is needed, the services of a competent professional should be sought.

Thank you for respecting the hard work of the author and the publisher. Your support of intellectual property rights is greatly appreciated.

Editor: First Editing, Dr. Vonda
Book Design: *the*BookDesigners

THE ULTIMATE GUIDE FOR LEADERS

ELEARNING GOLD

HOW TO ACHIEVE EXCELLENCE IN YOUR DISTANCE EDUCATION & TRAINING PROGRAM

Annette Levesque

Ontario, Canada

CONTENTS

Acknowledgments xi
Book Preface–A New World xiii
    A New Evolution in Education and Training xiv
    Reinventing Online Learning xiv
Introduction–In the Beginning. 1
    Unleashing the Power of Virtual Learning Globally . . . 4
    A Leader's Distance Learning Toolbox 5
    Transform Your Virtual Education and
        Training Program. 6
    What Makes a Virtual Learning Program Thrive? 8

PART 1
DEFINING YOUR VIRTUAL LEARNING GOALS 11

What Is Your Why? 12
Who Are Your Learners? 15
    Learner Demographics. 16
    Learner Self-Efficacy 17
    Skill Level and Learning Style. 18
    Interests and Goals. 18
Language of Instruction 20
    How Does It Affect Course Development? 20
    Effects on Collaboration 21
    Different Language Styles and Slang 21

Program Considerations for Adult Learners (Andragogy)....24
    Adult Learner Trends 24
    Learning & Training for Adult Professionals 25
    Knowles' Theory of Andragogy 26
    How Can You Apply These Principles in
        Virtual Learning?............................. 27
    Tips When Designing Virtual Learning for Adults.... 29
Learner Access to Technology 32
    Engage in Information Gathering 32
    Global Wi-Fi...................................... 34
    How Can We Adapt for Low Internet Speeds 35

PART 2

DIGITAL AGE LEARNING MODELS **39**

Blended Learning 40
    How Does It Work?............................... 40
    Benefits of Blended Learning..................... 42
Learner Autonomy 46
Creating Adaptable Learning Timelines.............. 52
    Adaptability Gives Learners Control 53
    Easier to Identify and Address Weaknesses 53
    Mastery Learning 54
    Antiquated Time Model vs. Achievement and
        Performance Assessment Models 55
    To Deadline or Not to Deadline... 56
    How Did We Create Adaptable Timelines for Learners? ...59

Digital Accessibility Requirements 62
    The Web Accessibility Initiative 62
    Web Content Accessibility Guidelines 63
    Legal Implications for Organizations............... 64
    Virtual Learning Accessibility Checklist............. 65

PART 3
FOSTERING COLLABORATION AND ENGAGEMENT......73

Interactivity in Virtual Learning.................... 74
    What Is Interactivity? 75
    Correspondence Courses vs. Interactive Courses..... 75
    Increased Engagement.......................... 76
    Learning Retention and Critical Thinking 77
    Collaborative Learning.......................... 78
Synchronous vs. Asynchronous Learning 80
    In the Beginning................................ 80
    What Is Synchronous Learning? 81
    What Is Asynchronous Learning? 84
The 7 Types of Interaction in Elearning.............. 89
Learning Communities............................98
    What Is an Online Learning Community? 98
    Why Build a Virtual Learning Community?.......... 99

PART 4
UNDERSTANDING LEARNING MANAGEMENT SYSTEMS..105

What Is a Learning Management System (LMS)? 106
    Bridging the Gap: Technology and Education Teams .. 107
    Balancing Investment and Effectiveness........... 109

    The Elearning Coach............................109
    Organization Size..............................110
    Who will Host and Maintain Your LMS?............111
Features to Look for in a Good LMS.................117
LMS Design Theme Considerations..................132
Common LMS Price Models........................144
    Pay per User Model.............................144
    Pay-As-You-Go Model...........................145
    Subscription Model.............................145
    The License Model..............................146
    Free Open-Source LMS Solutions.................146
Creating Your Elearning Test Environment..........151
    It Doesn't Always Pay to be First..................151
    Why Should You Have a Test Environment
        for Online Courses?..........................153
    An LMS Provider's Test Portal vs. Your LMS Portal...154
LMS Security & Privacy 157
    Website Hijacking..............................157
    Congratulations, You've Been Spoofed............158
    Blocking Foreign IP Addresses....................160
    Creating Multi-Level of User Roles................161
    The Human Element............................162
    Where to Store Learner Data?....................166

PART 5

REGULATORY LANDSCAPES & ACADEMIC FRAUD.......173

Managing Relationships With Regulatory Authorities ..174
    Create a Strategic Plan..........................176
    Meeting Standards Before Site Visits..............177

Build and Maintain a Relationship with
  Your Inspectors............................177
Communicate Openly and Honestly 178
Sometimes You Need to Check the Box...........179
Find a Champion–Join a Federation...............180
The Last Resort–Taking a More Assertive Approach . . 181
Academic Fraud.................................185
What Are the Most Common Types of
  Academic Fraud?............................186
Motivation for Academic Misconduct..............187
The Academic Fraud Autopsy 188
The Role of Academic History....................191
Creating a Culture of Academic Integrity 192
Academic Misconduct Disciplinary Measures 204
**Security Screening When Hiring Your Distance
  Learning Team 210**

PART 6

Creating a Distance Learning Strategic Plan 215

Why Do We Need a Strategic Plan? 216
**Getting Started–How to Create a Simple
  Strategic Plan (SSP)..........................221**
Step 1–The SWOT Analysis 222
**Step 2–Your Organization's Project Mission
  Statement 228**
Step 3–Your Core Values 232
Step 4–Vision Statement.......................238
Step 5–Review and Analyze Your SWOT 244
Step 6–Goal Setting........................... 248

Step 7–Your Action Plan..........................254
Step 8–Measurements for Success..................259

PART 7
FUTURE EDUCATION VIRTUAL CLASSROOMS AND BEYOND..................................269

The Future of Virtual Learning: What It Looks Like and Why We Need It..........................270
  Increased Hybrid Learning Models................270
  Greater Personalization.........................271
  Increased Availability of Virtual Reality............271
  Lifelong Learning 271
Artificial Intelligence (AI)
  Revolutionizing Education 272
  The Emergence of AI Chatbots...................272
  How Can We Use Future AI Tools to Benefit Education?........................273
  New Challenges Presented by AI 275

REFERENCES 281

Need More Help With Your Distance Learning Program?..............................286

ACKNOWLEDGMENTS

I am deeply grateful to everyone who has supported me on this incredible journey of writing this book.

First, I want to thank my amazing children, Jaden and Jared. You both inspire me every day to pursue my dreams. I also want to express my gratitude to my mother, Jennifer, for instilling in me the values of determination, perseverance, and resilience. Your unwavering belief in me has been the guiding force behind everything I have accomplished and everything I will continue to accomplish.

To all the incredible educators I have met on this journey, thank you for supporting my quest to innovate in virtual education. Two decades ago, your faith and belief in my vision gave me the unprecedented opportunity as a young educator to pioneer virtual learning worlds that transcended geographic borders.

I also offer my deep appreciation to my friends at the Ottawa Entrepreneurs Organization, who inspired me to think bigger and bolder in building global education. Your passion and dedication to driving innovation forward has inspired me every day.

Finally, I want to thank each and every reader who has taken the time to read this book. I hope this work inspires and empowers you to strive for greatness in your virtual education and training world.

PREFACE A New World

It was once predicted that the schools of the future would have no walls. However, no one envisioned this prediction becoming an overnight crisis-response reality in reaction to the global pandemic, which began in 2020. During the pandemic and its aftermath, a significant shift occurred in how humans now exist and co-exist on our planet. Much of our bricks and mortar learning and working environments has now migrated to some form of virtual world. Entrepreneur professionals, employees, schools, higher education institutions, and governments have found themselves in a whole new world, racing to keep up with the rapid advent of online learning.

The crisis-response migration of education and training methods has created many challenges for organizational leaders. Without the preparation, professional development, or experience typically required for such a massive global learning and training systems shift; many organizations find themselves trying to create or manage rapidly launched elearning environments comparable to the Wild West, where anything goes. Or does it?

A New Evolution in Education and Training

Teaching in a virtual world during the global pandemic has been a trial by fire for many schools and organizations. Instructors and students have often had to learn about what works in a virtual learning environment by also, unfortunately, experiencing what doesn't work. The pandemic teaching of 2020 and 2021 was not really distance learning nor really homeschooling—it was crisis teaching (Fisher et al., 2021).

Organizations and educational institutions which in the past have utilized solely physical classrooms now need to immediately be able to compete with existing online learning establishments. This also means being able to offer their education and training in some form of a virtual world. Businesses that have evolved into having more employees working from home or shifting to several remote days per week similarly need to provide effective virtual learning environments for team connection and training.

Reinventing Online Learning

As the health crisis now recedes or at least becomes manageable (hopefully for some time to come), we have more time to reflect on what we've created and be more intentional with the forms of education and training we are developing and offering in our new virtual worlds. Present-day focus can now be directed toward how to design, redesign and build elearning education and training programs, resulting in rich and engaging learning communities for our organizations. It is evident that we cannot return to the world as it was before. The global health crisis has encouraged many industries and nations to reconsider how they do things. It has provided the education and training sector with an opportunity to re-imagine education and how it's delivered, moving beyond how things were done in the traditional classrooms of the past to creating new solutions for a drastically changed world.

Learning has also changed for K-12 students who now find themselves at differing competency levels in all programs of study—dependent on how well their home locales and school boards fared education-wise during the crisis. To return to the semester-by-semester course structure and force students to continue into programs of study for which they are wholly unprepared is to deny one of the lasting implications of COVID-19: the need for change.

The pandemic experience has imprinted on all facets of our lives, including the traditional way professionals, university students, and K-12 students accumulate the number of credits needed to graduate from degree programs (Linney, 2020). It has presented institutions and educators across the globe with the opportunity to reinvent how they deliver education and explore newly evolving teaching technologies. Post-crisis, we now have the time to evaluate how we have adapted to deliver our education programs while using evidence and established best practices to determine what should come next and how best to utilize an unprecedented availability of new virtual worlds.

INTRODUCTION
In the Beginning

When I began pioneering elearning 20 years ago, my unusual combination of qualifications seemed to be that of a unicorn in new distance education learning environments. With university degrees in business and education, I found myself fascinated by new technologies at a time when many teachers were nearing retirement. In 2001, if you were a teacher and knew how email attachments worked, it immediately designated you as your school's new tech expert. The apparent gaps in bricks-and-mortar education and training systems also fascinated me. Why were schools only able to offer math, English, and science courses? What about students interested in psychology, business management, or horticulture? Often only five students wished to take business management, and administrators had to fill each classroom with 30 students to maintain instructor and school budgets.

As a young teacher embarking on my career, I needed an additional qualification course to teach international marketing and merchandising. The course was not available in my local city, and the closest university offering it was eight hours away. I was already teaching full-time, so leaving my job to move eight hours away to take one qualification course for a semester was impossible. After some research, I discovered that some universities offered online qualification courses—a completely new venture. I found the course I needed and started a journey that would forever change my education career.

As an adult student who was also a professional teacher navigating a newly pioneered elearning system at Western University in Canada in 2001, I was utterly fascinated. Being able to communicate with my professor and colleagues at whatever time suited my schedule was incredible. I could also work on my qualification course in the evenings and weekends outside my full-time teaching duties.

My natural entrepreneurial brain began to dream about a new model of learning for high school students. Specifically, I began pondering the possibility of gathering a group of twenty students from diverse schools throughout the city and placing them in an online classroom to study courses their schools could not offer—for example, business management or psychology. As the idea grew in my mind, I speculated on what might happen if we could gather students from across the province to fill an online classroom. Across the country? And then ultimately across the world!

The possibilities seemed endless. Why not have online courses for students who wanted to take a course their local school could not offer? What if we created online classes for students who required a different learning pace or who had a learning disability and needed more

Introduction: In the Beginning

time to study the material? Why were we testing students on material they could not master because of inflexible classroom deadlines?

I also pondered if online courses could benefit students away from school for a short period because they were training as athletes or experiencing a life crisis. They could pause their learning during their absence and then pick up right where they left off upon return a few weeks later. And finally, there were also adults like me who wanted to upgrade their qualifications or needed to take additional courses of study because they were changing career paths.

People who were actively employed professionals did not want to go back to attend an adult high school or college classroom in their 30s, 40s, and beyond. A distance education option could be an efficient and practical way for them to upgrade their qualifications. They could continue employment in their work setting while supplementing their learning needs with a single distance education course online. Learning virtually, they could expand their horizons to meet other colleagues and learners outside of their company, locale, and even their country.

These thoughts and many more led me to create a proposal and subsequently pioneer and launch my region's first high school distance learning course in 2001. And thus, my journey of learning as a distance education professional began.

ELEARNING GOLD—ANNETTE LEVESQUE

Unleashing the Power of Virtual Learning Globally

Fast-forward 20-plus years and one Master's degree in distance education later, and my reach as a virtual learning edupreneur and architect has transcended borders. I have collaborated and consulted with leaders of both public and privately held organizations, as well as institutions in Canada, the US, Antigua, Malaysia, Egypt, Nigeria, Russia, Beirut, the Dominican Republic, and beyond. I founded and grew two of the leading distance education schools in Ontario, Canada, in 2002 and 2005. Fourteen years later, both were acquired by one of Canada's most prominent international boarding schools.

These fantastic experiences have equipped me with unparalleled insights into the diverse virtual learning needs, challenges, and opportunities that organizational leaders encounter in today's rapidly evolving education and training landscape. This book is designed to share these insights to help leaders make informed decisions and assess the virtual education and training programs they offer. I want to help you unlock the full potential of virtual learning for your organization and create lasting positive change in education and training spaces worldwide. Together, we can embark on a journey to excellence in distance education—one that is sustainable, inclusive, and tailored to your organization's unique needs.

Introduction: In the Beginning

A Leader's Distance Learning Toolbox

As successful organizational leaders in this world, we typically fulfill two roles within our education and training organization: We create and build to prepare for our organization's future, and we react to events born of chaos and instability that affect us.

Many education and training organizations now have distance-learning systems in place. Some may have developed and launched their system before the global health crisis. However, in reaction to the pandemic crisis, many had to make their systems available to learners without the time and planning which would typically be allocated to such a massive new project.

Organizations are now reevaluating their virtual learning systems, which may have been established as a reactionary measure during the world crisis. The goal for many is to transition from surviving the global health crisis to thriving beyond it with a distance-learning program built to last.

You may still be in the phases of contemplating, developing, or launching a new online distance education and training program for your organization. Or you, too, may have been forced to rapidly establish an elearning program in response to the global health crisis. In either scenario, you have undoubtedly discovered or are discovering that setting up an online distance education program can be a complex and costly venture.

This book will provide you as a leader with the distance learning toolbox you need to create policies and strategies for excellence in your distance learning program. Whether you are launching a new virtual learning world or seeking to transform your current one, I will help you create a solid plan for building, launching, or relaunching your distance education program based on sound practices designed to help you achieve operational excellence.

Transform Your Virtual Education and Training Program

It is my goal to give you the information and tools you need to easily evaluate what features of elearning technologies are essential for your online education and training program and what free technologies and resources you can use to support your efforts without drastically and unnecessarily increasing your distance education budget. Some foundational areas which are explored include:

1. **Virtual Learning Success Criteria**–the most important things to consider when creating a virtual education and training program. What exactly do you need to know to get started? What are the most effective learning models used by distance learning programs today?

Introduction: In the Beginning

2. **Reducing Attrition Rates by Fostering Active Student Engagement**—how you can ensure learners feel engaged in your program and are an active part of your learning ecosystem to reduce incomplete courses and attrition rates.

3. **What Leaders Need to Know About Learning Management Systems (LMS)**—What you need to know *(but only what you need to know)* about choosing an LMS - especially if technology is just not your thing. What are some of the most important LMS features to consider for your program? What questions should you be asking your tech team?

4. **Managing Academic Misconduct in your Virtual Learning Program**—examining the different types of academic misconduct and how to address them. We'll take a look at how to create a culture of academic integrity in your distance education program.

5. **How to Plan Your Virtual World Launch or Update**—how to create a strategic plan with your team to successfully launch or update your distance learning program.

6. **The Future of AI and Chatbots**—how emerging AI Tools can benefit your distance education program and some of the new challenges these tools present for education programs.

What Makes a Virtual Learning Program Thrive?

Whether you are in a leadership role responsible for education and training in government, a corporation, a university or college, or a K-12 school, your responsibilities and the challenges you find yourself faced with have likely changed quite vastly in the past few years.

Many of today's leaders have been launched into extreme situations requiring them to undertake distance learning programs without planning or preparation. You don't need to be a technology guru to lead your team in creating an excellent online education and training community. So many new technologies are available today that it is impossible for even those working in the field to master them all. What we need to know, however, is why some distance education programs thrive while others suffer from low enrollment, high attrition rates, and student and staff dissatisfaction.

Final Thought

Ultimately, although the process of establishing a successful virtual education and training program can be demanding and complex, this book will help you simplify, recognize, and address these challenges head-on. It will help to guide you in reevaluating the strengths and weaknesses of your virtual learning program while providing you with the strategies your organization needs to become a leader in distance education and training. As you gain more experience and understanding in this realm, you will become increasingly confident you are making well-informed decisions to meet success requirements and best serve the needs of your learners.

1
DEFINING YOUR VIRTUAL LEARNING GOALS

What Is Your Why?

Whether it be a degree for students or a new certification for employees, offering your education and training program online is a necessity if you want to stay competitive in the digital age. But how do you go about designing and launching an effective one? In this chapter, we'll cover the essentials you will need to consider when deciding the type of elearning program your organization will offer.

Most organizations in the past few years have been deeply affected in one way or another by a rapidly changing world in a health crisis. Innovative technologies were already evolving at a pace likely challenging for you as a leader to keep up with and plan for. Most people today starting professional qualification or degree programs in technology are studying software and systems which may no longer exist by the time they graduate from their program.

Whether you're a university, a college, a high school, or a corporation providing education and training for your employees, there are many benefits to making education and training available online. I loved Simon Sinek's book *Start with Why* (2011), and it inspires me to ask why you feel it's important for your organization to offer your learners a virtual education and training program. Why should you build an elearning system for your company, and why is it essential to have a digital component to your education and training program? Are you already a school and need to transform your bricks-and-mortar learning program into a distance education environment? Is your organization already offering face-to-face classroom training or upgraded career qualification courses, and it's been forced to go online rapidly because of the new post-pandemic world?

A key question to ask yourself is why you need to go online. What is your purpose and reason for existing in a virtual world? What value proposition do you need to be able to offer your program participants to achieve program success, and what are the benefits of having an elearning system? Some examples might be:

1. **Remote Learning** – connecting with your learning system from home;

2. **Learning While Traveling** – having students or employees able to access your education and training while traveling;

3. **International Access** – connecting and training people in other countries; or

4. **Flexible Pacing** – allowing users to learn at their own pace using a competency-based learning strategy.

Whether your current education and training program is in a face-to-face classroom or online, these are typical questions I would ask an organization prior to constructing their elearning plan and strategy.

Define Your Objectives

Before you design your online learning program, it's important that you take some time to define your objectives. What are your goals for the program? Are you interested in offering an online degree or diploma program to students? Increasing employee retention or improving customer service? Boosting sales? Or something else entirely? Once you have a clear idea of what you're trying to achieve, you can start thinking about how best to design your program.

No matter your reasons for wanting to offer an elearning program, there are some key factors you will need to consider before transitioning. Defining your why and your organizational objectives for your program is an important starting point in ensuring your exciting new virtual world will meet the needs of your learners.

Who Are Your Learners?

As an organizational leader, you know that having a successful distance education program requires more than just a quality curriculum. It also requires understanding the needs and interests of each learner enrolled in your program. As you begin imagining your program design, it is important to know who your learners are and to design a program that will best serve their education and training needs.

Organizational leaders and instructors responsible for distance education program planning must consider learner demographics, psychographics, and language capabilities in their program design. Who are your learners, and what is motivating them to enroll in your program? Do they need to have taken a previous certification or hold prerequisite knowledge before taking your courses? Understanding learner motivation is a key component in developing and offering successful distance education programs.

For example, the worldwide health crisis prevented learners from accessing traditional classroom learning systems, thereby forcing a major shift to technological learning paradigms. As a result of this shift, many learners who would not typically seek out distance education and training solutions found themselves reluctantly entering a sphere of education that was previously foreign to them.

Additionally, when someone takes an online course, they typically have a set of expectations about the outcomes they will have attained after completing the program. Why should your learners attend your elearning program? What benefits will be derived from it? What will your learners expect to have achieved upon successful completion of your program?

If your online program covers an entirely different set of information, skill sets, and outcomes or delivers irrelevant information, they will be disappointed. Providing information that is relevant, relatable, and real-world-centered is critical to program success, so it's important to learn as much about your learners' expectations as possible (Pappas, 2018). If you can uncover individuals' motivation for enrolling in an elearning program and their end goals, you will be able to develop stronger elearning content and system processes to meet their needs.

Learner Demographics

Age, race, ethnicity, gender, marital status, income, education, and employment are all demographic considerations for program planning and learner success. Are your learners teenagers or adults, and how will this information impact the amount of support required to successfully complete your program? Are they Millennials? Gen Z? Boomers? For example, young teenage learners who enter foreign distance education programs usually want to earn a globally accepted pre-university diploma to enable them to apply for entrance to top universities around the world. International distance education learners typically do not seek to graduate from secondary school programs so they can go into industry to work. Among the thousands of international students I've worked with, the majority usually enrolled in distance education programs with a specific career goal in mind, with the most popular professions being medicine, dentistry, and engineering.

Adult learners, by contrast, are often seeking to further their education and training at universities and colleges or within their organization of employment in order to become qualified in a new career or to advance their knowledge and skill sets in their current vocation.

Learner Self-Efficacy

More and more studies have now examined the role of psychological factors and their impact on learner success. One such factor, known as self-efficacy, involves confidence in one's ability to achieve personal and professional goals. Self-efficacy is related to our sense of self-worth or value as a human being. Several studies have noted self-efficacy to be a significant predictor of academic success (Bressler et al., 2011). Although learner self-efficacy and learner motivation are deeply entwined, they remain two separate constructs. Self-efficacy is based on one's belief in one's own capacity to achieve, while motivation is based on one's desire to achieve.

Skill Level and Learning Style

You should also consider the skill level and learning style of every individual enrolled in your courses. Different students learn in different ways; some prefer visual content, while others are better auditory learners. Additionally, some professionals may already be advanced in their field, while others require more basic instruction. Once you know your learners' preferences, you can create courses that cater to their individual needs, allowing them to progress through the materials at their own pace.

Interests and Goals

Finally, it's important to understand the interests and goals of each person enrolled in your courses. Knowing what motivates them can help you tailor curriculum around their specific interests and aspirations so that they can get the most out of their learning experience. Taking time to get to know each learner on a more personal level is also beneficial for creating a sense of community within your virtual classroom world, and this is essential for successful distance learning programs.

Conclusion

As organizational leaders, it is our responsibility to make sure our distance education programs are tailored specifically toward our learner population's needs, interests, skill levels, learning styles, ages, locations—the list goes on! Having this information allows us to create virtual worlds which meet our learners where they are so that they get maximum benefit from our courses.

Leadership Questions

1. What are the values, opinions, attitudes, activities, interests, opinions, and lifestyles of your learners?

2. What impact might this information have on your distance learning program planning considerations?

3. Why are learners choosing your distance education program in particular, and what is motivating them to go online? For example, more opportunities for foreign university admission, exciting learning and career advancement opportunities, or perhaps just no other available options.

4. What prerequisite knowledge or credentials (if any) must a learner have to successfully participate in your program?

Language of Instruction

Language is a powerful tool, especially when it comes to online learning. It can be the difference between success and failure for any online learning program. When language is used effectively, it helps create an enjoyable and engaging environment for students, encouraging them to stay focused and learn more.

How Does It Affect Course Development?

When developing a curriculum for international distance education programs, most often, the language of instruction (typically English) may be a second or third language for the students taking part in the program. For example, an interview I conducted with Malaysian teachers and program coordinators in a Malaysian pre-university distance education program showed that a learner's background experience in English often played a significant role in their success. Malay is the official language of instruction in public schools in Malaysia, with English most commonly used for business communications. Malaysian students enrolled at our school would study their entire program in a secondary language. This was valuable information for me as an organizational leader, for our instructors, and for our entire elearning team.

Language plays a vital role in online learning programs. It makes up the entire communication framework between students and instructors and between students themselves.

One of the main reasons language is so important is because it allows learners to better understand what is being taught. If there's a problem with comprehension, chances are that learners won't be able to get the full benefit from their studies.

Effects on Collaboration

Another reason language is essential in online learning programs is because it helps promote learner collaboration. Without an effective way to communicate with one another, learners will have difficulty working together on projects or assignments. This can lead to misunderstandings and even conflict between learners if not addressed. This is especially true if proficiency levels in the language of instruction are vastly different between learners working on a group project.

Also, if English is the primary language of instruction, but another language is spoken by some learners, they may feel more comfortable using their native dialect to communicate with their peers.

Different Language Styles and Slang

In my experience working with international schools, learners who came from an English international school often did better in distance education programs. In contrast, those who came from a non-English school tended to struggle.

Learners also often struggled with differences between the style of English used in their home country and the style of English used in Canadian curriculum development. This can be true even for those whose first language is English. For example, English-language references in Canada can differ vastly from those used in the United Kingdom. I've watched British TV shows where English words are used that I have to look up because I've never heard of them. For example, the word "brolly" in British English means umbrella. The same term is not used in Canadian and American English.

Different languages can also have unique tones and levels of formality, which can affect how learners feel about their educational experience. Online courses for international learners thus need to be designed with language considerations in mind.

Conclusion

Language of instruction vs. the native language of international learners is a crucial consideration when designing your distance education and training program. It can affect the ability to facilitate comprehension among learners, promote collaboration among classmates, and create an enjoyable atmosphere for students while they learn.

Leadership Questions

1. Is your program of instruction a first or second language for your target participant group (i.e., English)? How much exposure to the language of instruction have learners had in prior studies?

2. Are there any literacy requirements that your program participants must meet?

3. When translating courses into other languages, will your organization's academic supervisory officials be able to review and monitor course content if they don't speak the language of instruction themselves?

4. Will there be any special keyboard or technology requirements to participate in your program in another language?

5. If your program is designed for younger learners, do their parents speak English or the primary language of your organization?

Program Considerations for Adult Learners (Andragogy)

We can define adult education as learning and its associated activities designed for those whose age, social roles, or self-perceptions define them as adults. The practice of teaching and educating adults may take place in the workplace or through more formal education in universities, colleges, and vocational programs.

As organizations continue to look for ways to reach their employees and adult learners, creating an effective distance education program is becoming increasingly important. While designing any distance education program requires attention to detail, there are some special considerations you will need to take into account if you are developing a program for adult learners.

Adult Learner Trends

In my 14 years of managing a high school distance education program, I would estimate that approximately 15% of learners enrolled in our virtual accredited high school program were adult learners. Some of the adult participants in the program had decided in their youth to leave their local high school program before completing it. Others were adults already engaged in a career who wished to upgrade their current position or qualifications. They typically required a science or math course that they had not taken with their original diploma.

All the adult participants enrolled in high school credit courses had one thing in common: They did not have the time or desire to take the academic credits they needed in a face-to-face classroom with younger learners. They wanted to discreetly complete their courses online so they could move forward in their lives and careers.

Learning & Training for Adult Professionals

Many of today's adults work as professionals in a knowledge economy where intellectual capital is king. They must often engage in systematic and sustained self-educating activities to gain new knowledge, skills, attitudes, and values designed for career advancement and self-improvement.

There are many different forms of adult education available through virtual learning today, with a variety of purposes:

- **Enhanced Career Opportunities** – professionals pursuing specialized qualifications for career and economic advancement to achieve financial independence;

- **Updating Qualifications** – persons who have already completed a university or college diploma and wish to upgrade their qualifications for career advancement through additional courses and learning;

- **Finish Incomplete Education** – mature learners seeking to return to school to earn a high school diploma that was never completed;

- **Developing Skills and Trades** – adult learners seeking vocational training to secure a qualification in a specific trade;

- **Personal Growth** – adults enrolled in general-interest courses to further their knowledge base and enhance their personal growth.

Knowles' Theory of Andragogy

Malcolm Knowles is widely regarded as the father of adult learning. Adults learn much differently than elementary and secondary school-aged students and are motivated by different factors. Mature learners are relevancy oriented and must understand the reason for learning something. Learning has to add value to their work or other life responsibilities to be of importance to them. Knowles outlined six fundamental principles he determined to have a critical impact on the adult learner:

1. **It's Contextual** – adult learners need to know why, what, and how;

2. **Learner Autonomy** – they want to be autonomous, self-directed, and manage their own learning—they need to be involved in the planning and evaluation of their instruction;

3. **Builds on Experiences** – the adult learners' prior experience is an important consideration when planning learning activities;

4. **Relevant Learning** – readiness to learn depends on the learner's needs: Adults are most interested in learning subjects that have immediate relevance to and impact on their career or personal life;

5. **It's Engaging** – orientation to learning is problem-centered and contextual and should engage critical thinking skills rather than be solely content-oriented;

6. **Core Benefits** – motivation to learn is based on intrinsic value, and there must be a personal benefit to the learner.

How Can You Apply These Principles in Virtual Learning?

When embarking on a virtual learning program with adults, it is important to explain any benefits of the material to be learned, why it is essential, and how it will add value to their professional and personal lives. For example, learning a new technology might increase organizational efficiency, which will in turn, increase profitability and employee wages. Or maybe it will help an employee advance quickly to another career level in the company. Providing a sound rationale and benefits is the key to gaining adult learner interest and commitment in your virtual learning program.

Since adults are self-directed, activities should aim to create elearning experiences that offer minimum instruction and maximum autonomy; they should allow learners to discover things and gain new knowledge for themselves, with instructors providing guidance and help when obstacles are encountered. When designing online course content for adults, there is a need to explain why specific concepts are being taught and ensure learning activities are task and problem-solving oriented (rather than of the type that promotes rote memorization). Learning material selection should consider the wide range of different backgrounds of learners and allow for different levels/types of previous experience. One way to achieve this is by allowing learners to choose course projects which reflect their interests and needs and have real-life applications.

It's also important to accommodate the busy and demanding lives of adult learners. They don't like fluff or "busywork" in their studies. They want to know what they're supposed to learn and then get straight to learning it. There's no need to try to impress them with special effects or outlandish animations; instead, instructional designers must impress them with great content.

Tips When Designing Virtual Learning for Adults

Flexibility

Flexibility is one of the most important considerations when designing a distance education program for adult learners. Adult learners have more commitments than younger students, such as work and family responsibilities. They may not have the ability or desire to commit to traditional class schedules or programs that require too much time or effort. It is necessary to give adult learners the flexibility they need to succeed by offering courses with adaptable scheduling options, remote access, and self-paced learning opportunities.

Content Relevance

As discussed earlier, adult learners are looking for relevant and meaningful content. When creating a distance education program for adult learners, the focus should be on providing content relevant to their current life experiences, job roles, and professional development goals. This will help keep them engaged and motivated throughout their studies. Online courses should provide adults with skills they can use in their current careers or help them transition into new roles within their organization or field of study.

Support Services

When creating a successful distance education program for adult learners, providing adequate support services is key.

Support services can include things such as online tutoring sessions; student counseling services; technical support staff available 24/7; webinars on topics related to the course material being studied; or even live video classes with instructors who can answer questions in real-time. By making sure necessary support services are available to your adult learners, you can ensure they get the most out of your program and succeed in their studies.

Conclusion

Creating an effective distance education program for adult learners requires careful consideration of unique needs which must be met for success. Flexibility in terms of scheduling and content delivery methods, relevance of content, and necessary support services are all critical components of any effective distance learning program for adult learners. By taking these considerations into account when planning your courses, you can create engaging experiences which provide value and meet the needs of your learners while helping them reach their full potential.

Leadership Questions

1. Will your education or training program be intended for adult learners?

2. Will these learners seek to complete a high school, university, or college diploma or upgrade an existing professional qualification?

3. How can you adapt your program to address adult learners' specific needs and learning relevance criteria?

4. What flexibilities can you build into your distance-learning program to accommodate busy adult schedules and lifestyles?

Learner Access to Technology

After you have established a clear idea of who your learners are, where they live, and why they will opt to take part in your program, it is imperative to gather some information on the technology they are using and their Internet capabilities.

For example, suppose a significant portion of your learners live in remote or developing regions which do not offer high-speed Internet connections. You will need to consider this if you plan to incorporate heavy video loads into your program design. When working with organizations that were building elearning programs, I have noted that unless a program was being offered to a specific group of individuals accessing it from a single location (i.e., corporate training center, bricks-and-mortar school, or learning center), one needed to be prepared to accommodate varying technologies with varying Internet speeds.

Engage in Information Gathering

In the early days of elearning, when our schools began offering academic credit programs to students enrolling from other countries, our staff conducted an information-gathering interview with teachers and program coordinators at partnering schools. This was very helpful in obtaining a deeper understanding of our learners and their technological capabilities. For example, some countries endured rotating power outages which could affect students taking

Defining Your Virtual Learning Goals

tests in their online courses. Unlike course lessons, in which a student could resume working when the power returned, a secured test permitted only a single opportunity to access it. Thus, a power outage would result in volumes of learners contacting our school to have their test reset so they could continue. This was only an occasional annual occurrence in Canada and the US, so it was an accepted inconvenience; however, in a country with several rotating power outages daily, it's a next-level problem.

Advance information gathering was so valuable to our program design that I began traveling each year to visit partner schools in geographic regions, cultures, and countries vastly different from our own. Many wished to partner with our academic program to offer it to their own students. I discovered some fantastic things; for example, in Malaysia, I learned that most students would access our Canadian distance education program from their local school, as very few had a computer or tablet in their home. If they tried to access their online course from home, it was typically using their mobile phone. We had some learners even trying to take tests using their mobile phones. This also presented many problems, as many test components didn't seem to function or reliably appear as they should on some mobile devices.

To my great astonishment, I also discovered some learners in Malaysia who wished to attend our program but lived too far from a partnership school to travel there every day. They wanted to access our online program so badly that their parents secured hostels near the schools for them to stay at during the week. This drastically affected both when and how learners could access their online courses to complete homework or study. It also affected the amount of home support available to them while completing our courses.

Typically, this meant we had to adapt our online academic program to ensure low bandwidth content access options were part of our course design. Some examples included:

- adding optional features such as text-only downloads;

- audio downloads (a fraction of the size of HD video learning); and

- breaking down larger course components into smaller ones, making them load more efficiently on mobile devices, especially over cellular networks.

Global Wi-Fi

Access to quality and reliable Internet is easy to take for granted, as high-speed Internet access is almost omnipresent throughout much of the Western world. I have neighbors just 20 minutes from Ottawa, Canada, whose attempts at obtaining high-speed Internet are the equivalent of trying to find a warm water beach in the Arctic. If you intend to offer your distance learning program in various geographic regions, it's important to recognize that there is limited access to high-speed Internet in many parts of the world. In many developing countries, mobile cellular networks are still the primary and sometimes the only way for learners to access an Internet connection. According to the 2021 International Telecommunications Union (ITU) mobile network coverage report, there are still significant rural populations who only have access to basic 2G cellular networks. Learners attempting to stream music and video on a 2G network or to load media-rich websites will experience frequent agonizing levels of freezing and buffering. Alternatively, however, instant messaging apps tend to work quite well. Thus, as you embark on developing your program design, gathering as much information as possible about your learners and their technological capabilities is extremely important.

How Can We Adapt for Low Internet Speeds?

There is a growing need for educators to provide online distance education and training to students who are living in geographic regions with low Internet speeds. It may initially seem like a daunting task, but adapting your virtual program for users living in these areas can be done with a few simple tweaks.

The first step is to understand the technical challenges that you are facing. The speed at which you can deliver digital content over the Internet will vary depending on the user's location and method of access. Tech team members should research specific areas and consider factors such as user technology, local infrastructure, and user habits. This will help you identify the gaps between your current offering and what users in these areas need.

1. Optimize Your Digital Content for Low Bandwidths
Once you have identified the issues, you can start having instructional designers and instructors optimize your digital content for low-bandwidth learners. This could include using smaller images or videos, reducing file sizes, or compressing data so it can be delivered quickly over slower connections. Streaming services such as YouTube or Vimeo may be worth considering as an alternative to traditional downloads. Streaming services allow users to access content without waiting for large files to download completely before they can use them.

2. Use Non-Technical Solutions Where Possible
Sometimes non-technical solutions may also help overcome low Internet speeds. For example, if you provide course materials via email or a website, you could send out physical copies of these materials instead of relying on digital delivery systems. Alternatively, you could use other methods of communication, such as phone calls or video conferencing tools (e.g., Skype or Zoom), instead of live streaming services if bandwidth constraints are an issue.

Conclusion

Adapting your online distance education program for learners living in areas with low Internet speeds can be challenging in today's world. By understanding the technical challenges, optimizing your digital content, and exploring non-technical solutions where possible, your organization can ensure your programs remain accessible even in geographic regions with limited bandwidth.

Leadership Questions

1. Will the participants in your online education or training program access it from a single controlled location or various geographic regions?

2. Approximately what percentage of your learners will have access to high-speed Internet connections?

3. What types of technology devices will your learners use to participate in your program?

4. Will you be required to offer low-bandwidth content as part of your program design? If so, what strategies can your team use to break down course materials into smaller images and file sizes?

DIGITAL AGE LEARNING MODELS

ELEARNING GOLD—ANNETTE LEVESQUE

Blended Learning

Have you ever heard the term "blended learning" and wondered what it means? In this section, I will explain what blended learning is and why it's becoming increasingly popular in organizations of all sizes.

Blended learning combines traditional classroom instruction with online learning to create a hybrid education experience. The idea is that both modalities work together to give learners a more comprehensive education or training experience. This could include anything from lectures followed by short quizzes or assignments posted online to courses delivered mostly or entirely online.

How Does It Work?

Blended learning combines synchronous and asynchronous virtual learning and classroom delivery. Well-designed blended learning programs unite the advantages of face-to-face learning with the convenience and modern tools of virtual learning, resulting in superior education and training programs. A blended learning approach can free important classroom time to focus on other learning. It allows organizations and institutions to enhance their current education and training delivery systems and enables learners to complete or upgrade their education using elearning technology. The best thing about blended learning is that you don't have to choose just one way of doing it—you can design a delivery model tailored to your organization's needs.

One of the most exciting and successful blended learning models I have worked with involved creating partnerships with international schools offering Canadian elearning programs. International learners would attend a partner school with a local foreign teacher supervising their Canadian distance education studies. The foreign teacher would provide cultural and technological support, face-to-face planning and organization, and academic support for each learner. The Canadian teacher handled instruction and learning materials in the distance education classroom. They also facilitated discussions and conducted all assessments and evaluations for learners. In this partnership, learners could receive the local support they required and instantly access advanced learning courses that were unavailable in their home country.

Blended learning models are my favorite of all online course design models. These models can vastly improve the learning experience, increase connection and engagement, and reduce program attrition rates. They allow organizations to take advantage of the benefits of both virtual learning worlds and personalized interactions in a face-to-face classroom.

Benefits of Blended Learning

The benefits of using a blended learning model to deliver your education and training program are numerous. For starters, blended learning allows individuals to learn at their own pace since they can access materials online anytime. It also will enable instructors to individualize instruction for each student, which isn't always possible in a traditional classroom setting. Other benefits of blended learning include:

Reduced Learner Anxiety – simulations in a blended learning environment can allow new staff and employees to become familiar with materials and technologies before entering the classroom. This can reduce the stress associated with learning an abundance of new material in a group environment. Simulations can be as simple as an online guided tour or as in-depth as an experiment where the learner can perform simple steps in a guided way. Simulations can teach concepts in a way that allows students to engage in new learning at their own pace. This can reduce learner anxiety while also helping learners who are absorbing and understanding new material at a varied rate.

Advance Preparation Time – prior exposure to learning materials in a virtual environment can give learners the confidence that comes with being exposed to new software or learning materials before attending an in-person class. Using self-managed quizzes and inventories, instructors can understand and measure each learner's progress prior to exploring topics in more depth in the classroom setting. This ensures all learners have the same necessary prerequisite information and understanding to discuss and explore more detailed and complex learning information in the classroom.

Immediate Curriculum Feedback – 24/7 access to self-managed assessments can also be an invaluable tool when finalizing a curriculum. If learners take a quiz after completing a learning module, and the majority experience difficulty with a section, this indicates that there may be a quiz content problem vs. a learner problem. We have a saying in education: If one learner performs poorly on a test, they perhaps didn't complete the materials or study for the test. If 80% of the learners perform poorly on the test, we must look very hard at the test and related learning materials. Thus, if many learners are struggling with an area of a course, online assessments can provide specific information and data to course instructors and designers in immediate and measurable ways. This allows them to adjust their presentation of the learning materials and address any problem areas, thereby enhancing the effectiveness of the education and training program.

Assessing Learner Readiness – online assessments and quizzes can test and ensure each learner has the required prerequisite knowledge and competencies prior to beginning a new education and training program. This can be especially beneficial for mature learners who have been away from the educational setting for an extended period.

Increased Instructor/Learner Communication – in a strictly virtual learning model, learning can sometimes feel isolated with only technological interactions. A blended learning model presents an increased opportunity for learners to connect with their instructors. They can connect via email, progress reports, or message boards, thus promoting several effective means for teachers and students to become more engaged with one another.

Increased Access to Learning Materials – in traditional education and training programs, learning materials were only available during classroom hours. Learners may have been able to take textbooks home with them, but acquiring any new resources required trips to the library. In a virtual classroom, learning materials are available 24/7.

Conclusion

Blended learning offers schools and organizations a way to efficiently teach students and employees while providing a high-quality educational experience. With its combination of traditional and digital teaching methods, blended learning gives instructors the flexibility they need to personalize instruction for learners—and helps employers maximize their training budgets. With new blended learning models and other technological advances, learners now have the benefits of both worlds. They have the flexibility to access and engage academia and their instructor from home while still receiving face-to-face learning and support for complex learning concepts. Ultimately, in today's world, I have found that blended programs consisting of both synchronous and asynchronous learning components offer the best learning opportunities. They balance learner connectivity and community with scheduling and learning pace flexibilities.

Leadership Questions

1. How can your distance education and training program offer blended learning opportunities to your course participants? What types of advance materials can you provide to your learners in your virtual world before they begin each module of study?

2. What self-assessment activities can your instructors provide to your learners to measure their course progress?

Learner Autonomy

Autonomous learning is a process that encourages and enables learners to take responsibility for their learning. Promoting learner autonomy in the design of your organization's elearning program can enhance learners' experience and be a major driver of learner engagement. But how can you create this in a virtual learning setting?

In many ways, enabling an autonomous learning model transforms the role of the elearning instructor to that of a facilitator or coach, thus allowing students to create and follow their own learning journey. One of the simplest ways to encourage learner autonomy in your program is to ensure various choices are available to your course participants.

It doesn't matter what age we are or what phase of life we are in. The availability of options in our learning program will increase our sense of autonomy and commitment to our studies. For example, when we can opt to research and write from a choice of course projects, it allows us to select an option that we feel we are interested in and is relevant to our current interests and place in life.

At the same time, we can feel great relief that we didn't have to complete a project option we would have deemed a snooze-fest. Choices increase our sense of control, engagement, and commitment to a learning program while also increasing feelings of satisfaction after completing a course.

The ability of your learners to chart their own course on their new education venture is an invaluable asset when setting out a learning strategy. Some benefits to learners include:

- cultivation of a keen sense of independence;
- an increased sense of intellectual curiosity and a hunger for knowledge that isn't always found when following an over-prescribed or dated learning model;
- a think-outside-of-the-box mentality that fosters innovation and critical thinking (Canonico, 2020).

By providing your learners with the opportunity to decide on their path toward their learning goals, you empower their decisions and allow them to embark on their own learning adventures.

The Intersection of Autonomous Learning & Technology

Autonomous learning intersects with technology in a few obvious ways. When the tutelage of an instructor does not constrain the learner, they're free to use the tools and technologies available to them for maximum benefit. A sound learning management system (LMS) will allow your learners to build personalized learning paths, track and monitor their learning progress, and self-assess their performance. The very nature of online learning also permits the shift in the instructor's role to instructor-as-facilitator to "check-in" on learner progress as requested or necessary.

Organizational and institutional leaders can leverage their learning platforms to encourage and foster autonomous education and training by considering the following:

Content Availability – making learning materials available anytime, anywhere, and using any technology, whether a PC, Mac, or mobile device. Learning materials must be available to learners whenever and wherever they need or want to access course content and work reliably on their chosen devices.

Using Relevant Materials – it is important to provide materials and resources relevant to your learners' demographics and needs. For example, if you deliver learning content designed for K-12 students to adults, you're going to miss the mark. When content is not relevant to the learner and their needs, dissonance occurs, resulting in learner disengagement. Relevant, meaningful activities which engage students emotionally and connect with what they already know help build learning connections and new knowledge. Make sure your LMS will allow you to design your elearning program to present the right courses and content in the right way and to the right audience. Learners should be able to access a wide range of relevant learning opportunities to create compelling learning experiences.

Digital Age Learning Models

Engaging Content Wins – while not all course material will be exciting, it's important to establish a content engagement experience that equates to more than flipping through a slide deck. For example, video now plays a more significant role in course development thanks to its ability to increase learner stimulation. However, not all learners will have access to the Internet speeds required to access video, so you must have appropriate media alternatives if you have learners living in remote locations or developing countries.

Provide Collaborative Social Learning Opportunities – where learners can discuss and share content with others. Creating collaborative spaces such as discussion forums, chat rooms, and other popular social networking applications in your LMS can allow students to exchange ideas, ask questions, and get feedback from one another. This type of peer-to-peer interaction can be very beneficial for autonomous learning because it helps learners develop critical thinking skills and encourages them to take ownership of their work. It's important to create ways to engage learners that allow them to participate in active, learning-focused conversations with their peers. Doing so will ensure you are not only building online courses but establishing a learning community for your organization.

Make it Easy to Use – enabling learner autonomy requires leveraging a learning platform which is not only easy to use but also user intuitive, putting the learner at the center of their learning journey. If users cannot easily navigate the platform, they most likely won't seek out learning content beyond what their instructor has assigned them.

Encourage Self-Assessment – once individuals understand the goals and objectives of a course, they should be encouraged to use self-assessment methods to evaluate their progress. Self-assessment allows learners to gain insight into their strengths and weaknesses. Instructors can provide students with tools, such as quizzes or reflection questions, to help them assess their performance.

Conclusion

Autonomous learning is an essential skill for all individuals, but it can be especially challenging in an online environment. Encouraging learner autonomy within your LMS revolves primarily around championing a sense of ownership. If individuals feel empowered to learn and understand the benefits, they will be inclined to seek learning opportunities independently. For a learner to take charge of their learning or have the desire to do so, your instructional strategy must instill confidence, independence, and self-sufficiency (Canonico, 2020). By encouraging self-assessment and collaboration amongst learners, instructors can create an environment that supports autonomous learning in your virtual distance education and training program.

Leadership Questions

1. In what areas of your courses can you offer choices to your learners?

2. Is your course content available to learners 24/7?

3. Are you using relevant and engaging learning content which is interesting for your category of learners?

4. Are your courses and content readily accessible for learners to interact with and navigate?

5. Do they function well on a variety of different mobile devices?

Creating Adaptable Learning Timelines

Creating adaptable learning timelines for individuals can make all the difference in how they learn, allowing them to set their own pace while still staying on track with your program. In this section, we'll explore why adaptable timelines are beneficial and how they can benefit your organization's virtual education and training program.

One of the major benefits of distance education programs is that they can operate on a continuous enrollment basis; learners do not have to be limited to specific school start and end dates. In comparison, in a bricks-and-mortar classroom model of study, there is often a standardized semestered reporting time for evaluating all learners (especially true of K-12 school systems and universities).

The need for static reporting timelines (usually attached to provincial and state funding models) almost always supersedes an individual's education needs. This can create inequitable educational opportunities for learners. Anderson (2011) affirms, "The ideal learning environment aims to develop the learner's independence and facilitate the learning process by providing supports that are flexible, accessible, and readily available when needed" (p. 419).

Adaptability Gives Learners Control

One of the most significant advantages of creating adaptable timelines for learners is it gives them a sense of control over their learning experience. When individuals have the freedom to learn at their own pace, they can create a timeline that works for them and allows them to develop skills at an optimal rate. Adapting the timeline also allows learners to focus on topics that are more challenging or require more attention without feeling rushed or overwhelmed. When a learner achieves the goals and outcomes for their course (as prescribed by the program they are attending online), they earn their course credit or certification.

Easier to Identify and Address Weaknesses

Another advantage of flexible timelines is that it is easier to identify and address any challenges in an individual's performance when completing tasks or understanding topics within an elearning program. This allows instructors and mentors to quickly identify areas where additional help is needed, leading to better overall results from participants in the program. When students have the freedom to work at their own pace, they naturally gravitate toward areas where they need further guidance and practice.

Mastery Learning

This leads us to the concept of mastery learning, a transformational education and training innovation of our time. At its core, mastery learning enables learners to move forward at their own pace as they master knowledge, skills, and concepts. Unlike conventional classroom instruction, where a course continues to move forward each day (regardless of whether a learner is ready), in mastery learning, a student masters one concept before proceeding to the next. This can be especially beneficial in courses requiring a cumulative understanding of concepts, for example, math or accounting. Effective implementation of the principles of mastery learning in elearning programs can completely change how students learn, how instructors teach, and how education and training programs work. It can transform how we develop curriculum, design courses, measure learning, and train instructors (Ellis, 2020). Flexibility in learning tempo can provide all learners with a fair opportunity in course evaluations, regardless of whether they require timeframe accommodations to complete their online course. This is of benefit to:

- individuals with special learning needs;
- those who are being treated for other medical, emotional, and psychological conditions;
- those in developing countries without regular access to learning materials and technologies;

- and adult learners juggling their learning with work schedules and the ongoing demands and responsibilities of family life.

Antiquated Time Model vs. Achievement and Performance Assessment Models

In the early years, when we were launching the first accredited online private high school in our region, it wasn't easy to receive approval from our local Ministry of Education to deviate from the standard semestered learning model. The government held fast to the idea that learners must attend 110 hours of class time to legally achieve a high school credit. This concept worked in a face-to-face classroom model for learning where attendance could be easily tracked. However, this requirement was almost impossible to confirm in the world of online learning.

Zoom did not exist, and the only way to monitor student attendance was via their login times. This was a highly unreliable statistic, as a student might leave the computer to work offline or to continue reading their textbook. Conversely, they could also log into their course, thus starting the statistical login clock, and then leave to make lunch. Login times on their own could not accurately reflect time directly spent on teaching and learning. Additionally, some learners may have had prior knowledge, which enabled them to achieve the course outcomes at an accelerated pace. Transferring the face-to-face attendance model to the world of elearning deemed advanced learners ineligible for their course credit if it took them less than 110 hours to successfully complete their course.

In the end, we had students themselves complete learning log sheets recording their time spent working on their course and submit them as part of their course credit. As an educator, the entire process seemed ludicrous to me since students could creatively complete their log sheets to meet the 110-hour requirement. However, it seemed to satisfy the Ministry of Education inspector by checking the box to meet the attendance legality requirement so we could move forward with our program. Unfortunately, as most of us in leadership positions are intimately aware, logic and government regulation are rarely symbiotic partners.

To Deadline or Not to Deadline...

In the spirit of making the move to providing adaptable timelines for learners, many education organizations are now considering the abolishment of antiquated hard deadline models. However, they face many challenges when trying to turn this new ideology into a reality. The most common obstacles that arise include:

1. How do we staff instructors for courses for undefined periods of time? How do we adapt our funding models?

2. At what point does a flexible timeline become a detriment to learners in terms of material recall before final learning evaluations?

3. How do we deal with instructors and advocates who feel that learners are not being taught the skills necessary to deal with "real-world" deadlines?

4. What if a course with active learners in it changes or must change because of new learning requirements, curriculum, or regulations during a learner's "extended study period?"

These questions and many more arise as we consider major paradigm shifts in program design for today's education and training models.

In our first school, described earlier, shifting to flexible learning timelines in online courses (during elearning's infancy) was deemed to be an outlandish venture. There was much pushback at the proposal for this new learning model. Beyond the inability to track student attendance, it was just an extremely unpopular idea amongst government officials, education inspectors, administrators, and even face-to-face classroom instructors. Education officials were apprehensive about not keeping traditional reporting timelines for student marks. They were also concerned about the lack of ability in existing statistical education reporting technologies to accommodate flexible learning timelines. It's now 2023, and many government technological systems still aren't capable of appropriately collecting and reporting elearning student data (but that's a different chapter altogether).

Organizational management was concerned with how we would create a plan and budget to fund staff and instructors for learners enrolled in courses for an unknown duration of time. Instructors themselves were untrained and unprepared to conduct learning in a virtual world. For many, this new world represented a change far beyond their comfort levels with technology.

Given that we developed this model 18 years ago and were essentially pioneering elearning, there was also a great deal of apprehension from other educators. They felt students needed to learn to juggle responsibilities and deadlines, the perception being if we did not strictly teach them this, they could never deal with deadlines and responsibilities in the real world. With adult training, there was a perception that if an adult could not commit to completing learning materials within prescribed timelines, they would not be successful in their envisioned career.

And last, when it came to government-mandated curriculum changes, Ministry of Education inspectors were initially 100% hard-line-in-the-sand not going to accommodate delaying implementation of new curricula for elearning courses. This time was required to give educational institutions an opportunity to build, test and launch rich and engaging courses. Failure to provide transition times to build and launch new curricula remains a problem for many K-12 schools in Ontario today.

How Did We Create Adaptable Timelines for Learners?

Given that we were a school in a privately funded, accredited K-12 education organization, we thankfully had some flexibility in how we negotiated funding models for both learners and instructors. Since our courses were tuition-based, we devised a solution whereby students would pay tuition to fund instructors for only the time they needed to complete their studies. They would initially pay tuition for a three or four-month course (selecting the option they felt best suited their timelines). If, at the end of the three or four-month study period, a student required more time in their course to complete it, they could subsidize and extend their instructor time for 30 days. Conversely, we compensated instructors for the number of students enrolled in courses with them each month. This both eliminated issues with timelines and permitted the accommodation of varying class sizes.

If learners needed to pause their participation in an online course for an extended time because of special life circumstances, medical needs, or other reasons, they could do so. However, if learners were absent from their course for too long, memory recall for academic concepts and materials became an issue. We thus determined that the maximum flexibility we could provide in our specific program design, which would give balanced benefits to students, was one year to complete their course. On average, however, in the absence of exceptional circumstances, most learners completed their course within 4 or 5 months.

The Failure Fallacy

The argument that learners will not be prepared for real-world consequences if we do not fail them in their youth for the non-completion of assignments is a fallacy. Teaching learners to continue toward an objective even if they have missed a deadline is the best real-world lesson we can provide to prepare them for life.

The Ministry of Education in Ontario, Canada, separates the idea of academic knowledge/skill/critical thinking evaluations from learning or study management skills (i.e., meeting deadlines), and I like this concept. Just as with life skills gained over time and with experiences, study management skills for students mature at different paces. Just because a student cannot meet deadlines when they are 14 or 15 does not mean they cannot gain the skills to become an autonomous learner at age 18 or 19. As educators, we must provide them with the opportunities to do so.

In my experience, people are very accommodating in the real world when you need more time to juggle multiple life responsibilities. Learning in today's world is a lifelong journey, and we live in a knowledge economy. We must give students, adult learners, and professionals the different accommodations they require in their learning place and their learning pace so that they can access valuable ongoing educational opportunities. We must enable learners to *keep going* as they encounter life's inevitable hurdles on their learning journey.

Conclusion

Continuous enrollment and adaptable timelines are two features of distance education courses that give students a sense of control over their learning experience. These elements are essential because they allow learners to focus on topics which are more challenging or require more attention without feeling rushed or overwhelmed. Mastery learning is another aspect of distance education which enables learners to move forward at their own pace as they master knowledge, skills, and concepts. By taking advantage of these three features, distance education programs can provide a high-quality and personalized learning experience for each course participant.

Leadership Questions

1. Will your distance education and training program have fixed course start and end dates?

2. What flexibilities can you build into program timelines for your learners?

ELEARNING GOLD—ANNETTE LEVESQUE

Digital Accessibility Requirements

No matter where you live in Canada, the US, or another nation, you've likely noted that web accessibility is becoming an area of greater focus for governments and organizations. It is surprising to learn that the number of North Americans who identify as having a disability is growing. In Canada, for example, one in five people aged 15 years and older have reported having at least one disability that limits their everyday activities. This figure is up from 13.7% in 2012 (Morris et al., 2018). However, despite the growing prevalence of online tools for persons with digital accessibility requirements, many websites and elearning programs have overlooked the needs of these learners. It's important to educate and inform ourselves on the diverse needs of our learners so we can become leaders in inclusive and innovative elearning education design.

The Web Accessibility Initiative

The Web Accessibility Initiative (WAI) was founded in 1997 by Tim Berners-Lee, the inventor of the World Wide Web. It is an international consortium that works on improving web accessibility standards for people with disabilities. It is composed of a group of experts from all over the world who work together on developing web standards for everyone, regardless of disability or tech level. The ideology is that anyone should be able to access websites, irrespective of physical or mental disabilities, gender identity, race, ethnicity, etc.

Web Content Accessibility Guidelines

WAI has developed international Web Content Accessibility Guidelines (WCAG) and educational resources for organizations to help make their websites and digital content more accessible to people with disabilities. WCAG outlines how websites should be designed and developed so everyone can use them without extra effort or accommodations. It also provides guidance on how developers and designers can create new features or content types that will also be accessible across all platforms and devices. They developed the guidelines in cooperation with individuals and organizations worldwide to provide a single shared standard for web content accessibility that meets the needs of individuals, organizations, and governments internationally (W3C, 2023).

WCAG divides into three levels: A, AA, and AAA. Level A consists of basic requirements such as ensuring text contrast is high enough for users with visual impairments; ensuring images have alternative text descriptions; providing video captions; and more. Level AA expands upon Level A requirements by adding keyboard navigation support, language identification tags for multilingual websites, audio description tags for audio content, etc. Level AAA includes even stricter standards, such as time limits being removed from automated process steps, descriptive labels being provided when using data tables, and more complex usability considerations, such as avoiding animation entirely if it could cause seizures in users with photosensitive epilepsy disorders.

Legal Implications for Organizations

Federal accessibility legislation is now becoming law, and there is a growing public awareness and demand for digital inclusivity. In the U.S., the Americans with Disabilities Act (ADA), which was passed in 1990, has increased access and opportunity for people with disabilities in the US. It's a piece of legislation that affirms the civil rights of people with disabilities and places inclusion at the forefront of the law. In 1998, the U.S. Congress also amended the Rehabilitation Act to require federal agencies to make electronic and information technology accessible to people with disabilities. Section 508, which is both a law and a standard, helps eliminate barriers in information technology (GSA, 2020).

More recently, in Ontario, Canada, as of June 30, 2021, public-sector organizations, businesses, and organizations with over 50 employees must legally comply with website and digital learning content standards outlined in the Accessibility for Ontarians with Disabilities Act (AODA). Organizations with fewer than 20 employees developing digital education and training content for public-sector and large-scale organizations will also need to make these standards part of their product development plans. All websites and web content must also comply, including mobile apps (web-based applications). Larger entities must establish and maintain an accessibility policy and strategy and make it publicly available on their website. They must also provide accessibility training to employees, volunteers, and those who provide goods and services on behalf of the organization (Thomson, 2018).

When building your elearning program, you must know any federal or provincial guidelines for your region to ensure you abide by the law and create barrier-free access to your virtual content. This will also safeguard your organization's reputation as one that believes in an inclusive digital presence for all.

Virtual Learning Accessibility Checklist

The report *Include everyone, keep everyone: Your guide to web accessibility in Canada* (2021) provides a suggested digital content checklist derived from some of the primary principles outlined in WCAG. As part of your organization's style guide and course inspection checklist, I recommend including a section on accessibility requirements. I have adapted this list into four sections below to help get you started.

1. **Visibility** – can everyone see and view your digital content?

- Can all users (those with full vision, low vision, or no vision) make use of assistive technologies (screen readers, zoom magnification, high contrast tools) to view what is being presented in virtual lessons and materials?

- Are you using high contrast between text and background colors? Color alone should not be used to convey a message, symbol, or instruction.

- Do images contain alternative text?

- Is the text legible using a font size of at least 16pt (avoiding overly small font sizes)?

- Are fonts, buttons, and icons scalable?

- Do videos provide closed captioning or text transcripts?

- Are web pages designed with a meaningful sequence and logical order?

- Is there sufficient color contrast for text, images, and icons?

- Is there a standardized color theme throughout courses that adheres to the organization's style guide (more on style guides in the section on designing learning modules)?

2. **Functionality** – are complete LMS functions and content accessible, allowing navigation by instructors and learners in a variety of ways?

- Can you navigate LMS functions, web pages, documents, and media fully using not only a mouse but also by using a keyboard, switch controls, and other devices?

- Are "skip-to" links provided to allow keyboard users to jump directly to a specific activity or section of learning content?

- Do digital pages contain titles or headings?

- Can learners start and stop media with a variety of controls (media is not set to auto-play)?

- Are captions provided for audio recordings?

- Do any external resources (such as videos hosted on YouTube) have closed captioning enabled so that learners with hearing impairments can still understand the content presented?

3. **Simple and Easy-to-Understand Interface** – can learners easily understand how to navigate and operate your virtual course website?

- Are all course information and instructions (including language and LMS interface operation instructions) simple for all users to comprehend?
- Are navigation and information placement consistent across courses?
- There are no unclear or confusing error messages.
- Abbreviations are not overused.
- Do buttons or controls contain labels?

4. **Universal Device Compatibility** – can all devices reliably access and navigate your distance learning website?

 - Is content developed using current and up-to-date technologies?
 - Can a wide variety of user agents (PC, Mac, mobile devices, and tablets) interpret LMS functions, course materials, media, and tests?
 - Can you view and use content with a range of popular Internet browsers?
 - Is your content compatible with commonly used assistive technologies, i.e., screen readers, page magnification, Braille displays, keyboards, and switch controls?

Conclusion

Despite being around since 1997, the importance of the Web Accessibility Initiative (WAI) and the Web Content Accessibility Guidelines (WCAG) has only increased with the surge in online learning brought on by the global pandemic. Ultimately, these standards provide a way for organizations to ensure their online learning experiences remain accessible to everyone regardless of ability or technology level. Governments have determined that legislation is critical for guaranteeing digital accessibility and inclusivity. Thus, it is essential to be aware of any requirements which apply in the areas you intend to deliver your education and training program. Adopting the principles outlined in WCAG will ensure your organization's online learning experiences are inclusive, resulting in a diverse population of learners participating in your virtual learning program.

Leadership Questions

1. Are there any special digital accessibility and inclusivity requirements you are legally required to observe in your country and industry?

2. Do you have a specialist on your team (or consulting with your team) with knowledge of WCAG to make your digital content more accessible to learners with disabilities?

3. What will you include on the virtual learning accessibility checklist for your organization?

3

FOSTERING COLLABORATION AND ENGAGEMENT

ELEARNING GOLD—ANNETTE LEVESQUE

Interactivity in Virtual Learning

When it comes to online course design, creating opportunities for interactivity is key. Interactive activities can help engage learners, foster collaboration, and build community. But why is this important? Why should you care about interactivity in the online courses offered by your organization? Let's take a look.

Have you ever been a part of a class where the instructor drones on and on for 1.5 hours? Or even worse, 3 hours in the case of a university course? They are talking "at" you the whole time vs. engaging you? And if you're lucky, they might show a slide deck or two during their lecture. I am now seeing articles published by professional doctors on topics like "How to stay awake during Zoom Classes or Meetings," outlining sincere strategies for staying awake, including "drinking cold water" and "chewing gum." Apparently, we no longer have to hide our gum under our desks as the instructor approaches during class. It's now required to stay awake.

Given that we have all had the experience of being bored to death in at least one course, I am completely mystified as to why many instructors have now transferred these same teaching methods to virtual education and training environments with the expectation of elevated learner engagement and success.

What Is Interactivity?

One of the most important characteristics of an effective elearning course is interactivity. There is a long history of research and acknowledgment of interaction's critical role in facilitating excellence in distance education. Within education literature, we use the term interaction in various ways to describe different types of exchanges between different participants and objects associated with teaching and learning. Wagner (1994) defines interaction as "reciprocal events that require at least two objects and two actions. Interactions occur when these objects and events mutually influence one another" (p. 8). Garrison and Shale (1990) define all forms of education, including that delivered through distance education programs, more broadly as interactions between learners, teachers, and content.

Correspondence Courses vs. Interactive Courses

I am now seeing many organizations offering courses incorporating wonderful media and video components to increase learner engagement; however, there is no real instructor present in the course, and often there are no other learners to interact with. These are not genuinely interactive elearning courses; they are essentially digital correspondence courses. If the learning in a course does not evolve and cannot be modified based on interactions between the instructor and course participants, it is essentially a static virtual correspondence course. Organizations need to note that course participants can feel very lonely in one-way interaction online courses, and the result is typically very high attrition rates.

Increased Engagement

Interactivity in online learning systems creates opportunities for learner input and engagement, thereby allowing them to become involved with the lesson content. It entails going beyond the passive one-way nodes of reading, listening, and watching static media content. When opportunities for interactivity are provided in elearning courses, we move from being passive observers on our learning journey to riding in the driver's seat.

By giving learners a chance to collaborate and share their thoughts with others, you can create a sense of community that encourages learning and discussion. Plus, interactive activities are often more enjoyable than simply reading through the material, so learners are more likely to stay engaged and pay attention during the course.

Vaughan, Cleveland-Innes, and Garrison (2013) maintain that designing collaborative and interactive learning and assessment activities fosters open communication and supports a healthy climate for collaboration. This in turn promotes trust and classroom cohesion in the distance education environment. "The key to engaging learners in deep and meaningful learning is through collaborative communities of inquiry–not the passive lecture approach that currently dominates higher education" (p. 99).

Learning Retention and Critical Thinking

When interactive elearning courses get it right, learners experience several positive outcomes. First, they retain the knowledge from their course at a significantly higher rate than those enrolled in passive courses. People are more likely to remember information if they have had some sort of interaction with it. By allowing learners to take part in discussion forums, group projects, and quizzes, you can help them retain more information than if they were passively reading through the material.

Second, learners build critical thinking skills by putting their learning to use in realistic scenarios. This requires them to think, interact with peers or an expert, and evaluate the outcomes based on the decisions they make. Learning also often occurs faster in interactive courses because learners work on higher-order thinking skills like appraising, interpreting, and summarizing information rather than merely labeling or memorizing information (Gutierrez, n.d.).

The Gen Z, Gen Alpha, and Net Generation (also known as Net Gen, the Google Generation, or the Me Generation) pose new challenges for educators. They represent a demographic of tech-savvy learners habituated to multi-tasking who expect to control what, when, and how they learn. They are a generation of smart, impatient, and creative learners who expect results immediately. The Net Generation are very often focused on themselves and heavily reliant on a variety of mobile devices to access various forms of learning (Hutchison et al., 2008). "To help address these challenges, educators are increasingly coming to understand that we must provide more interactive and engaged learning experiences" (Vaughan, Cleveland-Innes, & Garrison, 2013, p. 99).

Collaborative Learning

Exceptional elearning courses have the power to transform learning and content into meaningful interactive experiences for learners. They include content such as simulations, immersive tutorials, gaming, problem-solving sets, etc. Top-tier interactive content facilitates interaction between groups of learners while promoting active learning. It can include multi-person training simulations and synchronous distance learning, where variables set by one person's autonomous behavior impact others. This promotes experiential learning similar to learning in real social ecologies or situations.

Adding interactive elements to your online courses allows learners to learn from one another and from the material itself. This type of collaborative learning environment helps create a deeper understanding and will enable learners to benefit from each other's experiences and insights. It also encourages knowledge sharing, leading to further collaboration down the line.

Conclusion

Incorporating interactive elements into online course design has many benefits, including increased retention rates, higher engagement levels, and collaborative learning opportunities. By allowing learners to interact with one another and the material, you can ensure that your online courses are engaging, compelling, and memorable for everyone involved. When we facilitate opportunities for interactivity in elearning courses, participants can have a more enjoyable and effective experience. By considering how to incorporate interactivity into your elearning course design, you can create a learning environment that engages and excites learners in your distance education and training program.

Leadership Questions

1. What types of interactions should occur in the online courses offered by your distance education and training program?

2. How do you think increased interactivity will affect the overall quality of the online learning experiences provided in your courses?

3. What benefits could increased opportunities for interactivity have on your distance education and training program?

Synchronous vs. Asynchronous Learning

When considering the design of your distance education and training program, one of the most important decisions you will make will be whether to provide your program in a synchronous (real-time) or an asynchronous format (anytime). For example, should your instructors deliver lessons via Zoom or through recorded video sessions posted in online classrooms? In this section, we'll discuss the key differences between synchronous and asynchronous learning—outlining each format's benefits, drawbacks, and potential uses in your elearning program.

In the Beginning...

In the infancy of elearning, it was very difficult for schools offering international distance learning programs to offer synchronous classes. First, technologies with the ability to host online conferences, such as Zoom, Google Meet, Adobe Connect, or Microsoft Teams, did not exist. There were also many issues with groups of learners living in various geographic locations and different time zones and working with various Internet connection types and technologies. It was challenging for educators to figure out how to create a sense of connectivity and community between learners in a primarily asynchronous environment.

Course attrition rates were high, and students often felt lonely in their courses. We tried various strategies, such as creating an ecafé for students to gather in and interact socially within the school; however, for whatever reason, it never really caught on. We also offered live online office hours for instructors on Skype. Some students used the opportunity to interact with instructors in a live forum, while others did not. It was interesting to see that some students who attended Skype office hours did not always have questions about their course; often, they seemed to be there seeking a connection with their instructor. They wanted to know where their instructor lived and if they had a family or a dog, or their favorite food. This emphasized the importance of finding ways to create synchronous connections in the limited environment and technologies we were working with.

What Is Synchronous Learning?

Synchronous learning involves online or distance education sessions that happen in real time, often with a set class schedule and required login times. This means instructors and students interact in a specific virtual place at a designated time. In synchronous sessions, instructors commonly take attendance as they would in a lecture hall or classroom. Common types of synchronous learning include videoconferencing, teleconferencing, live chatting, and live-streamed lectures or tests, which are viewed or completed in real time.

Synchronous Learning – Benefits

Synchronous video-conferencing sessions provide regular opportunities for face-to-face discussion, individual guidance, and mentorship. Learners can interact regularly and frequently with their instructors and get to know them. Synchronous formats can be especially beneficial if an organization is beginning the transition from a traditional classroom to a virtual setting. Some of the other benefits of synchronous learning include:

- **Live Interaction** – it promotes active discussion between instructors and learners;

- **It's Instantaneous** – the availability of immediate feedback from instructors and peers;

- **Develops Learner Relationships** – it allows for personal interactions, which can reduce the sense of isolation in a course;

- **Remote Interactions** – it offers learners the comforts of home with no commute time;

- **Removes Physical Boundaries** – there are no geographic limitations for learning and meetings. Participants can join from various parts of the country or world.

Synchronous learning is excellent for team-building activities, quick Q&A sessions, and any other activity that needs to be done in real-time. This type of instruction is also ideal for allowing you to obtain instant feedback from learners or when you want to create an immersive experience that replicates a physical classroom.

Synchronous Learning – Disadvantages

That said, synchronous learning also comes with some drawbacks. The primary disadvantage of synchronous learning is that, like face-to-face learning, individuals must be available for learning sessions on a fixed schedule. No one can join late or leave early without disrupting everybody else's learning experience. Attending synchronous learning sessions may be challenging for learners who have opted for virtual learning because of hectic and unpredictable work schedules (TBS, 2021).

It may also be problematic if you offer your program to international participants and learners living in different time zones; 1 pm in an area of Canada or the US may be 1 am in Asia. If flexibility is the number one reason your learners have enrolled in your virtual program, then adapting to a heavy synchronous learning schedule may defeat the purpose.

Synchronous learning sessions can also be challenging for participants in low-technology or limited Wi-Fi access zones. Successfully taking part in a group video conferencing session typically requires at least 25 to 50 Mbps download speeds. For users in remote regions which do not provide unlimited Wi-Fi data access or who must connect using cellular data, the average group Zoom session can use 1 GB to 2.4 GB of data per hour.

What Is Asynchronous Learning?

Asynchronous learning is a type of self-paced online instruction where learners can access materials anytime and from any place with an Internet connection. It does not require real-time interaction between instructors and students. All materials required for reading, lectures, assignments, and exams are available in the online classroom. Typically, asynchronous virtual learning will include self-guided lesson modules, pre-recorded video content, virtual libraries, lecture notes, and online discussion boards or social media platforms.

Asynchronous Learning – Benefits
In asynchronous learning, course participants can access content when it best suits their schedules. This flexibility makes it perfect for busy professionals who need to fit their learning into their already-packed agendas. Some of the other advantages of asynchronous learning include:

- **Flexibility** – for adult learners with a demanding daily schedule, or who work shift work, and learners living in different time zones, asynchronous learning provides the most scheduling flexibility. Learners can complete a module on the train or bus ride to work, listen to a lecture on a headset while the kids nap, or work the night shift, sleep until noon, and then take a quiz over lunch. Learning materials and discussion threads are available through a virtual classroom website and are accessible anytime and anywhere.

- **Unlimited Review** – asynchronous instruction also allows learners to review materials multiple times if needed and gives them additional resources such as chat forums and discussion boards where they can connect and ask questions outside of live sessions.

- **Modified Learning Pace** – one of the most empowering features of asynchronous learning is that the learner can (for the most part) set the pace for their studies (usually within set deadlines). They can read and review materials as much as they need to understand and master the concepts being learned. There is also an ability to accelerate through the learning materials for rapid learners or those who already have some familiarity with the content being taught. Conversely, learners who require more time to absorb new knowledge can review information, take notes, and practice retention without worrying about falling behind or missing key points in a lecture.

- **Affordability** – education and training can be costly, and affordability can often be a consideration in learner program selection. Fully asynchronous programs are typically less expensive than synchronous programs, as instructors may serve on a part-time basis as subject matter experts (SMEs) and course facilitators. They do not have to provide real-time instructional hours. Online learning options such as massive online open courses

(MOOCs) also often carry a lower price tag because they don't require daily attention from instructors or administrators. Instead, students work through the content themselves, occasionally interacting with instructors through email or social media. Self-guided modules, video tutorials, and virtual libraries allow learners to pursue their education with minimal oversight and expense.

Asynchronous Learning – Disadvantages
On the downside, asynchronous instruction can sometimes lack immediacy if learners have questions or require assistance immediately (although chat forums help somewhat to bridge the gap). The primary disadvantage of using a program model that is comprised 100% of asynchronous learning is the sense of isolation the learner may feel. For many learners, courses that consist of 100% asynchronous learning can be a lonely experience.

Discussion threads and email can never be a substitute for real-time interaction with one's instructor and peers. Asynchronous learning is also far less collaborative than its counterparts: Opportunities to discuss, debate, and network are scarce (TBS, 2021). When a learner is truly stuck on a course component and needs support, solving a problem can sometimes seem overly complex and lengthy via email and text chat. It can also sometimes be more difficult for instructors to track learner engagement in asynchronous learning since students work on the course at different speeds. In this learning format, it is essential for instructors to provide timely feedback so learners stay on track.

Conclusion

Both synchronous and asynchronous learning have pros and cons, but ultimately, it all depends on what your organization needs most. If you're looking for an engaging way to get learners together quickly with minimal setup required, then synchronous might be best; however, if your learners need maximum flexibility, then an asynchronous course delivery format may be your go-to option instead. Typically, most education and training programs today combine the benefits of both synchronous and asynchronous delivery formats for various components of their courses. Ultimately, it comes down to finding what works best for your specific program. It's best to take some time to explore both options with your elearning team before deciding which one will work best for your organization.

Leadership Questions

1. What types of synchronous and asynchronous learning opportunities will your program provide to its learners?

2. Regular feedback is essential to overcoming any course obstacles and encourages learners as they progress. How and when will learners receive feedback from their instructor?

3. Will the feedback be synchronous or asynchronous, and what type of technological mediums will be used for feedback?

The 7 Types of Interaction in Elearning

In our ever-changing world, the way we learn has evolved too. Today, more and more people are learning online. But what does that mean for engagement? How do we keep learners engaged when they're not in a physical classroom? That's where interaction comes in. Do you know your options when working with course designers and instructors to create interaction models in your courses? What types of interaction should occur in your distance education and training program? Let's look at the kinds of interaction in online learning and why they are important.

Michael Moore (1989) first argued that the three most common forms of interaction in distance education are learner-learner, learner-teacher, and learner-content. Anderson and Garrison (1998) later broadened these categories of interaction to create an interactive structured model that included teacher-teacher, teacher-content, and content-content interaction (as cited in Anderson, 2011). In the new age of artificial intelligence, we now also have system-system interaction in virtual learning systems.

1. Learner-Learner Interaction

This is when course participants interact with each other. It is a vital part of any online course experience. In a bricks-and-mortar classroom setting, this interaction happens as learners listen to each other's comments, ask each other questions, and build rapport through frequency of face-to-face contact. In distance education environments, organizations must create formal and informal interaction opportunities in their course designs.

Kollof (2011) considered learner-learner interaction essential in building a successful learning community in any distance education environment. She stated it supports productive and satisfying learning and helps learners develop problem-solving and critical-thinking skills. Other learning research has shown students achieve more when they work together, socialize, and collaborate to finish their work (Anderson, 2011). Technologies to support learner-learner interactions are usually found in the course learning management system (LMS). Interactions can also be supported by other email and chat technologies such as Skype, WhatsApp, Signal, Telegram, Google Meet, and Zoom.

2. Learner-Content Interaction

In this type of interaction learners interact with the course material. Learners can connect ideas and concepts when interacting with content rather than passively reading information or watching videos. This could be as simple as taking notes during a lecture or taking part in an activity requiring learners to apply knowledge from the class material. By engaging with content, learners can gain a better understanding of the material and retain it longer than when passively absorbing information from lectures or slideshows.

Learner-content interaction has always been a primary component of face-to-face classrooms. Standard forms are reading a textbook or article, listening to a lecture, watching a video, or doing independent research in libraries. The Internet supports passive forms of learner-content interaction but also provides a wealth of new learning opportunities through virtual labs and experiments, learning objects, online quizzes, and online computer-assisted learning tutorials. The development of interactive content that responds to the way each learner behaves allows for the customization of content in unprecedented ways to support the needs of each unique learner (Anderson, 2011).

Learners can use the Internet to research and access up-to-date and relevant learning content and can communicate anytime with experts in each subject area they are studying. Social bookmarking websites such as Twitter, Pinterest, StumbleUpon, and Scoop are websites that allow learners to share collections of web pages, articles, blog posts, images, and videos and contribute to group projects. Blogs and technologies such as WordPress and Google Docs can facilitate learner self-reflection and peer review of course assignments. Learners can now use collaborative technologies to work together on things like summarizing course discussions, refining research papers, or even co-creating online books (Vaughan, Cleveland-Innes, & Garrison, 2013).

3. Learner-Instructor Interaction

This is when students interact with the instructor. This type of interaction is essential to successful online learning. Instructors should provide feedback on each assignment and be available to answer questions or offer guidance as needed. This helps learners feel supported and allows them to ask questions if they have them. It also gives instructors a chance to monitor progress and provide personalized advice or help when it's needed.

Learner-instructor interaction occurs in distance education classrooms using a wide variety of technological tools for synchronous (live, real-time) and asynchronous (non-live) communication formats between students and instructors. Some examples include instant messaging, video conferencing, email, discussion boards, live chats, and group presentation solutions such as Adobe Connect, Elluminate, GoToMeeting, and Zoom. Some exciting newer virtual world applications, such as Second Life, Oculus Rift, Croquet, Roblox Edu, and The Palace, allow teachers and learners to go beyond text-based and audio communication and collaborate synchronously in immersive 3-D worlds.

The new widespread availability of virtual communication tools can create an expectation in learners for an immediate response from their instructors. Anderson (2011) suggested instructors do not have to respond immediately to every learner's question and comment. They should instead play a less dominant role in overall classroom communications, thus supporting the emergence of increased learner commitment and participation. Vaughan, Cleveland-Innes, and Garrison (2013) affirm we should encourage learners to develop personal relationships and that setting guidelines is best done collaboratively to foster engagement and participation. They emphasize that it is important instructors do not dominate course discussions, as learners may feel intimidated and discouraged from expressing their thoughts and opinions.

This type of interaction allows instructors to get feedback from their learners so that they can adjust their teaching methods accordingly. For example, if a learner has an issue with an assignment or isn't grasping a concept, instructors can work with them individually to find out what's causing difficulties and come up with solutions.

4. Instructor-Content Interaction

This type of interaction occurs when instructors interact with the course material. It focuses on the instructor's content creation (solo or in liaison with an instructional designer/elearning team). This includes course modules, learning activities, writing articles, creating learning objects, composing lectures, recording videos, and creating discussion topics in asynchronous discussion forums. Instructors can use social networking systems such as Brainly, Litpick, TikTok, Classhook, Google Schools, Office 365, YouTube, and Edmodo to extend the physical boundaries of the classroom. They can create discussions and debates that include past learners, potential employers, and subject matter experts.

5. Instructor-Instructor Interaction

This is when instructors interact with each other. It creates opportunities for collaboration, professional development, and the fostering of interactive communities, furthering the advancement of best practices in global distance education programs. This can happen in faculty meetings, departmental meetings, or even casual conversations between colleagues. RSS feeds and social media websites such as LinkedIn, Twitter, Twiducate, Tween Tribune, EDU 2.0, Wikispaces, Google Classrooms, and Edmodo can also facilitate instructor interactions. These sites encourage teachers' awareness of knowledge growth and discovery within a scholarly community of their peers.

6. Content-Content Interaction

When the course material interacts with itself, it is considered content-content interaction. It is a relatively new concept and occurs when an LMS is programmed to interact with other automated information sources to continually update itself and gain new capabilities (i.e., wikis, blog posts, podcasts, news channels or live feeds from websites such as NASA, Twitter, or LinkedIn). This interaction provides learners with "just in time" information in addition to the static or fixed content uploaded by their instructor when initially creating a course. Social media applications also have the potential to support collaborative learning activities in content environments.

7. System-System Interaction

This is when the learning management system (LMS) interacts with other systems. For example, if an LMS integrates with a student information system (SIS), that would be a system-system interaction. System-system interaction can benefit learners in a few ways. First, it can ensure that there is no duplication of manual entry efforts on behalf of administrators and instructors. For example, if a student's information is updated in the SIS, that update will also occur in the LMS. Second, interactivity between systems can provide a more seamless experience for students. For example, if a student completes an assignment in the LMS, that completion can appear in the grade book in the SIS. And last, it can also create interactions between ecommerce systems and an LMS to automate enrollment systems so students can immediately access features and courses after paying tuition fees.

In our futuristic world, I would love to see system-system interaction evolve so that if a student is struggling to master a course concept and isn't doing well on assessment evaluations, the SIS, grade book, and content systems would interact to adjust the content being presented. A sample formula could be:

= if the student achieves less than 60% on a course evaluation → then the LMS produces additional modified content in that topic area to further assist the student in attaining learning mastery of a topic.

Or

= if the SIS shows a student is from the Arctic vs. the Caribbean → the LMS produces geography lessons relevant to that area.

A simplified version of this idea is already occurring in monster business systems conducting marketing surveys and client queries. The questions presented in a survey can evolve based on an individual's answers. Amazon's algorithms also adapt what products and books appear to users based on user interactions with their website. How amazing would it be if they adapted some of these technologies for global distance education programs?

Conclusion

So there you have it—the seven different types of interaction which can occur in your distance education and training program! Remember that these types of interactions are important and can contribute to successful virtual learning experiences for participants in your virtual education and training program.

Leadership Questions

1. What types of interaction will occur in your distance education and training program?

2. What types of interaction are missing from your current program or strategic plan that could enhance your virtual learning program?

Learning Communities

It is so important for people to feel like they belong to a community. People feel a need to find others with shared values and to feel as though they belong. We trust those with whom we can perceive common values or beliefs. For example, if you're a Canadian traveling to another country and you meet other Canadians, you immediately feel a bond when you meet because you're both Canadian.

When it comes to education and training, learning communities play a critical role. A learning community allows people to come together, discuss their ideas, and get the most out of the educational process. For organizational leaders seeking ways to improve their education and training program or increase engagement amongst students and staff, setting up a learning community is a great way to do just that.

What Is an Online Learning Community?

An online learning community is a group of like-minded individuals, whether they be business professionals, educators, or students, who come together virtually to collaborate and learn from one another. We can find these communities all over the Internet, on platforms like Facebook, Instagram, Twitter, Pinterest, or an organization's LMS. While they might be virtual, that doesn't mean they're any less supportive or powerful than in-person communities. Some might even argue that they are more so since they are not limited by physical geographical boundaries or time zones.

Why Build a Virtual Learning Community?

There are many reasons you should build an online learning community (if you haven't already). For one thing, these communities are incredibly supportive of individuals participating in an online education and training program. Whenever a learner has a question or needs some advice, there's sure to be someone in the group who can help them out.

The establishment of learning communities plays a critical role in education and training. Learning communities provide a virtual space for instructors, learners, and learning partners to align around a common goal. We want to be around people and organizations who are like us and share our beliefs. Effective communities connect people, organizations, and systems eager to learn and work across boundaries while holding members accountable to a common agenda, metrics, and outcomes.

Sharing Knowledge
Another benefit of establishing learning communities is that it allows knowledge to be shared more effectively among members. When learners have access to a wealth of knowledge from others in their group, they can benefit from different perspectives and approaches when tackling a problem or developing a solution. This leads to more

creative solutions that help all members reach their goals faster and more efficiently.

Learning communities allow learners to draw from each other's experiences and build on one another's successes and failures. As we all know, there's no better teacher than experience! By accessing experienced professionals within the same field, learners can gain valuable insight into how things should be done to achieve success.

Collaborate Without Geographic Boundaries
Learning communities enable participants living in different physical geographies and from varied backgrounds and cultures to share results and learn from each other. This improves their ability to achieve rapid yet significant progress on their collaborative learning journeys (Harvard University, 2015). They promote and value learning as an ongoing, active, collaborative process with a dynamic dialogue between all members. The shift to learning communities shatters the conventional idea of a solo instructor constructing their course, all guidelines and policies for learners, and then also delivering it to 30 learners online.

Learning communities are an essential tool in helping all members of the learning journey stay engaged and active in the educational process. An important advantage of building a community for your learners, instructors, and stakeholders is the virtual space it provides to explore, understand, interact, and improve teaching practices. Regular discussions can be held between instructors and stakeholders, centering on aligning the curriculum to learning needs, continuously improving instructional strategies, and enhancing education and training procedures.

A Sense of Belonging

Learning communities can provide a sense of belonging for learners. This increases their engagement and commitment to a course and collaboration with their peers. In an increasingly digital world, it can be challenging for learners to make meaningful connections with their peers. By establishing learning communities, learners can connect with one another in an environment where they feel comfortable sharing their thoughts and experiences.

Professional Development

Another substantial reason to provide a learning community for your organization is for professional development. It's the perfect way for members to stay up-to-date on what's happening in an organization's education and training program and to ensure they are always growing as professionals. It will provide a space for your team to share resources, try new strategies, and get feedback from their peers.

Opportunities for Virtual Fun

Finally, online learning communities can be a lot of fun! These groups provide a space to connect with and learn from like-minded people from all over the world. It is not uncommon for individuals to even make lifelong friends along the way, leaving them with a memorable and positive experience after participating in your education and training program.

Conclusion

Establishing learning communities plays an essential role in education and training because it provides learners with a sense of belonging, enables knowledge sharing among members, and allows them to benefit from each other's experiences. When you create a virtual learning community that fits what your particular learners are interested in, you'll put them into your ecosystem. This also gives you new opportunities to learn about them. Individuals who experience sociable, connected learning become more engaged in and out of the classroom community and increase their commitment to their virtual distance education program. This increases their potential for academic success.

Leadership Questions

There's a vast range in how an online learning community can scale, and understanding what type of virtual community will be most beneficial for your learners is the first step in building it. For example:

1. Is there an age range for your learning community?

2. What types of things in a virtual community will interest your particular demographic of learners?

3. Are you offering an advanced education and training program to a select group of learners who prefer a specific and more intimate community environment? Or are you offering a comprehensive international program for young learners worldwide?

4

UNDERSTANDING LEARNING MANAGEMENT SYSTEMS

What Is a Learning Management System (LMS)?

A learning management system (LMS) is a software application that provides the framework to handle all aspects of the learning process in your virtual learning ecosystem. You can think of it as an online home for your organization, where most of your educational activities will take place. It enables your organization to create and manage lessons, courses, media, quizzes, and other materials for learners and employee training. It also provides a platform where instructors and learners can interact with one another. A learning management system will help you deliver training materials to students and staff quickly and efficiently in a single, organized online space.

In business organizations, an LMS is typically used to deliver elearning courses and track employee progress. They are also used to manage in-person training events, such as conferences and seminars, and track attendance. LMSs vary in features and price, but all offer a way to manage and deliver employee education effectively. Many businesses choose to use an LMS because it offers a central repository for all employee training materials.

Have you ever gone shopping for a new cell phone and suddenly found yourself immersed in vast technological options you don't understand, and you have no idea which ones you'll need? There are many types of LMSs, and selecting one for your organization can feel quite overwhelming and seem overly complicated. The abundance of available LMS features can make it hard to decide which will be helpful to instructors and learners and which will be a distraction. The problem, in essence, is that you don't know what you don't know.

To help get you started on your LMS journey, this section will give you an idea of what features you should consider when evaluating and comparing your LMS options. You will want to discuss these items with your elearning consultant, elearning team, and any potential LMS provider.

Bridging the Gap: Technology and Education Teams

Over the years, I have noted that a consistent disconnect often occurs between technology people and an organization's education and training teams. Typically, it's because each team doesn't know what the other requires, and they do not understand the needs and limitations of the others' field. This disconnect can become a very expensive one when purchasing an LMS.

Educators know what they need to do in their courses and can articulate course education requirements, but they often need to learn what technological tools they require to create a community for their students in a distance learning environment.

There is a new generation of educators, exposed to technologies at a younger age, who may be comfortable figuring out how to use a new virtual classroom environment; however, when making selection decisions regarding system features and the hosting of their elearning environment, there is often a significant gap in the expertise and knowledge required to be the primary decision-maker in this process. If an instructor isn't aware of the possible features they can request for their online classroom, for example, the ability to send pre-scheduled messages to learners, how would they know to ask for it? They might ask how the grade book works, but why would they think to ask how often the system information is backed up and where backups will be stored? Does it back itself up automatically, or will some manual backup activities be required of your organization?

Conversely, tech people are not educators. They know how to build fabulous systems and technology but are typically entirely unfamiliar with the end-user experience or needs of the instructors and learners actually using the systems. A technology person or company who can set up and install a learning management system (LMS) but has never actually taught a course is likely unfamiliar with specific features educators may need to meet their course accreditation requirements. Although many free distance education LMS companies specializing in elearning technologies now exist, they rarely specialize in best practices and considerations for program and content development.

Balancing Investment and Effectiveness

As a primary decision-maker, it can be very difficult to know how much is reasonable to invest in your elearning LMS. What technologies will be easy to use and best serve the needs of your learners? Is the price of these technologies affordable, and can you manage the ongoing licensing fees to maintain these systems?

In today's fast-paced and ever-evolving digital world, executives and managers responsible for implementing and overseeing elearning systems are faced with a multitude of challenges on various fronts. For instance, how do you stay up-to-date with the latest innovations in educational technology and learning methodologies to ensure your virtual programs are not only competitive but also effective in meeting organizational goals?

Additionally, you will need to strike the perfect balance between approving user-friendly technology platforms and the budgetary constraints of your organization. Having someone regularly evaluate and compare different elearning solutions available on the market for you can be crucial to ensuring that spending on unnecessary features is minimized.

The Elearning Coach

At this juncture, it can be an excellent idea to bring in an elearning education expert on a short-term (or long-term) consultant basis to help you and your team evaluate your options. They can also coach you through selecting and setting up your virtual LMS. You will note I did not say to bring in a tech expert, as you will require someone who is *both* an expert in elearning technologies (the system) and an expert with ideally a Master's degree and specialty in distance education (the program and education tools required). Although there are many experts available to consult solely on elearning technologies, they cannot assist you in correctly assessing your technological needs if they do not also have a background in education. The common result is organizational leaders have technology companies present them with expensive large-scale solutions they may not immediately need or use. On the other hand, an excellent elearning systems and education consultant will coach you through selecting affordable technologies that fit both the size of your organization and its budgetary needs.

Organization Size

When evaluating your LMS options, one of the first questions is how large your organization is and how many users you expect to access your LMS at once. Some systems are large and complex and can be used by thousands of learners, while others are smaller installations accessed by only a handful of learners or employees for in-house training. You should consider not only your current number of users but also what you think your user growth might be in the next five years.

Who will Host and Maintain Your LMS?

1. Using an LMS Hosting Company
Who will host your LMS is a critical part of setting up your new virtual world. The answer to this question will depend on your available resources to host and manage your own system. Smaller organizations with several hundred users or even less than a hundred users usually opt to outsource the hosting of their LMS to a professional company that will maintain the LMS, perform updates, and troubleshoot any technical issues. This is a good option for an organization that does not have much experience with education technology and wishes to rapidly launch its distance and education training world. However, there can also be drawbacks to outsourcing the management of your LMS, including cost.

Outsourcing hosting can be quite expensive, as there is typically an initial setup cost, monthly maintenance fees as well as general fees when it is time to run a system update of your LMS. I've also worked with organizations that have many issues transitioning away from an outsourced host when wanting to take over their own system. It can certainly be done, but it can sometimes be a painful technological process.

You will also want to consider that the company you outsource to will typically host and fully control your LMS and its corresponding files. You will have to rely on them for all your needs, including troubleshooting if the system goes down or if users are experiencing any errors. For this reason, you will want to ensure that any company you outsource to has 24-hour live technological support available and is not just a Monday-to-Friday service center, as many smaller LMS hosts are. There's nothing more harrowing than having your system go down at a critical time of year and being unable to reach a human technical support person. System failures will always result in your users and learners flooding your phone lines, and it can be highly frustrating for your team if they do not have the in-house expertise to solve the problem and cannot reach someone who can help them.

For example, in my first elearning school, we outsourced everything related to setting up and maintaining our LMS. This was initially a fantastic experience, as we knew absolutely zero about what was required to run the system. Outsourcing to a company specializing in system setup allowed us to skip the learning curves and be up and running at the speed of light. However, as our school grew and our number of users and customization needs increased, we started encountering difficulties. Every September, on the first day of the school year, all of our learners would excitedly log in to our elearning system simultaneously to begin their first course (not only our learners but also the learners of every other organization that our provider was hosting), inevitably causing the system to crash. Can you think of anything worse than being a strictly elearning school, having your system crash, and being unavailable on the first day of classes for the new school year? It was catastrophic, and as we were calling our technical support provider, so was every other organization they were hosting; thus, no help was available to us.

This happened to us in two concurrent school years. We had a fantastic distance education school with unique and popular elearning courses that learners and our partner organizations loved. However, crashing on day one of the school year and having no power to rectify the situation was a significant threat to our image and brand. Accordingly, we eventually decided to invest in transitioning to host our own system.

The issues described above are not a problem with all outsourced hosts. There are some brilliant companies that can take care of your learning management system for you. The above notes are to guide you into what questions you need to ask any potential companies you are considering for outsourcing your LMS needs.

2. Hosting Your LMS Yourself
If you have a technology person in-house who can maintain your LMS, troubleshoot any glitches that may occur, and perform the technological updates when required, you may choose to take care of your own LMS hosting and maintenance needs. In this scenario, you would budget to subsidize one person's salary to perform these tasks. Whether this becomes a full-time role for the assigned technology person will depend on the size of your LMS and the number of users accessing it. Organizations with thousands of learners typically prefer to host their own LMS, as it gives them more control over the look and feel. It also allows them to troubleshoot any issues immediately in a crisis.

Hosting your own system also has pros and cons. Some pros are that you have complete control over your system, where the digital files for it are located, the look and feel of the system, and you can immediately make changes to the system if there's something you don't like (without having to write a plan and get a proposal from a provider to make the changes for you). If the system goes down or you're having technical issues, you can call your own staff tech at 3 am (although they won't love you for it), and you may have a better chance they will pick up the phone if the situation is dire. Essentially, you will have a lot more control when you are hosting your own system but also a lot more responsibility. This will also require committing to a part-time or full-time salaried position to fulfill your LMS hosting and maintenance needs.

3. Hosting via Independent Contractors (the middle ground)
A third option that may be the best viable option for organizations not quite ready to staff a full-time technological person to take care of their LMS is outsourcing the setup and maintenance work as needed to an independent contractor. This is typically a solo person working from home with experience in elearning systems and a great deal of general technical knowledge. They will provide you with an estimate for any work you require to set up, maintain, and run updates on your LMS. This is a good option if you only have a small number of learners accessing your system at any one time (as long as the world won't end if your site goes down and you can't reach your technological guy for half a day or so).

Conclusion

If you are looking for a comprehensive system that will provide the framework to manage all aspects of your virtual learning ecosystem, then a learning management system is what you need. It enables organizations and educational institutions to create and manage lessons, courses, media, quizzes, and other materials efficiently and effectively. By using an LMS, businesses can more effectively manage employee education and training, which can improve employee productivity and knowledge.

When evaluating your LMS options, be sure to consider how large your organization is and how many users you expect to access the system at one time. With so many distinct features and different systems available on the market today, finding the right LMS for your needs can seem daunting. However, armed with this knowledge of what an LMS can offer and some key considerations for choosing an LMS provider, you will be well on your way to finding the best solution for your organization's needs.

Leadership Questions

1. How large is your organization, and how many users will likely use your LMS in the next year?

2. How many users do you expect to access your LMS simultaneously (pressure on the system)?

3. What is your expected user growth in the next five years?

4. Do you have the resources to host and manage your own LMS, or will you consider outsourcing its setup and management to another provider?

5. What type of technical support availability will you require for the LMS users in your virtual world (i.e., 24/7 vs. next-day email support)?

Features to Look for in a Good LMS

Whichever LMS you ultimately decide to choose, its features will need to support the education and training goals you have outlined for your organization in your strategic plan. In this section, we will look at some features that make an LMS stand out from the rest and can help you get the most out of your virtual classrooms.

User Interface and Functionality

The user interface is essential because it affects how easy it is for instructors and students to navigate your system. Look for an LMS with a clear, intuitive design that makes common tasks, such as creating courses and quizzes, straightforward. The user interface should also be responsive so that it works well on any device, including smartphones and tablets.

LMS Dashboard

Information a learner first sees when logging into your learning portal is premium web real estate. This is the default homepage page in a learning portal, typically referred to as the dashboard. Your LMS dashboard is an essential tool for instructors and learners. It provides a centralized view of all LMS activities, making it easy for instructors and learners to monitor progress and identify areas for improvement. It should provide learners with specific details on their progress, new announcements from their instructors, and any upcoming deadlines.

Many users often do not immediately scroll beyond the main screen after logging into their courses unless they are looking for something specific, so any essential course-related items instructors want learners to immediately see should be located on their learning portal dashboard.

Menu Blocks

A menu block in a learning management system (LMS) is a feature that allows you to create a menu of links to grouped or specific content within the LMS. This can be useful if you want to create a custom homepage or navigation menu for your course. For example, you could create a menu block with links to all of your school policies or another block with external links to helpful online tools and resources which might help a learner throughout their course.

Most LMS courses are organized using blocks that load specific types of content or media into particular areas designated by the organization's LMS design. There are several types of standard LMS blocks, and if needed, each block type can be used multiple times on a page. For example, one kind of block might hold calendar data while another allows for news feeds.

Universal Documents Block

One way for organizations and institutions to ensure all students have access to important information about their virtual program's policies and procedures is to create a universal section or block that appears in all courses. This area can contain general information documents (template documents that apply to all courses) related to the following:

- school/organizational program policies, tools, and resources for all students;

- the code of conduct for the learning program, including appropriate practices for online communications in class discussions;

- your organization's privacy policy;

- helpful learning resources or tools and technologies for learners (i.e., MLA or APA citation resources and software, presentation software, online library access information, etc.);

- links to learner feedback surveys which are completed at predesignated points in the program and upon completion or exit from the program;

- troubleshooting tips and whom to contact for technical assistance.

Instructor Information Block

There should be a clear and easy-to-find block containing basic instructor information along with their email, phone, and virtual chat information (Skype, WhatsApp, Signal, or Telegram, etc.) for online office hours. A regular schedule for virtual and synchronous class sessions should be indicated. Including a photo of the instructor will add a personal element to the course.

Calendar

A course calendar feature is a necessary organizational tool for students and instructors. It should communicate and display important events and deadlines related to the course. This will help learners plan their work and ensure they complete it on time. There are different types of events that the LMS calendar should be able to display:

- **Global Events**: these events apply to all learning portal users in all courses. When a global event is added to the calendar, it should be viewable in all online courses. Permissions to create global events are typically given only to your organization's site administrators.

- **Course Events:** the instructor creates these, and they are viewable solely by the learners enrolled in a specific course.

- **User Events:** an instructor or student creates these, and they are viewable only in their own profile.

Announcements

An announcements area or block is an LMS tool that allows the instructor to create an essential first point of contact, a starting place for students every time they log into the classroom. And because the course announcements section is usually located centrally in a high-visibility area, it's important to use this real estate for more than just a weekly greeting or dry rundown of course policies and procedures. Having a robust set of announcements in a course is one way to enhance instructor presence in the classroom, leading to heightened learner engagement and the building of rapport. Instructors can use this area in their course to deliver just-in-time logistical broadcasts or concentrated bursts of instructional content to expand on underlying themes (Pritts, 2020).

Course Enrollment

The enrollment needs of your organization are important to consider when evaluating an LMS. The LMS you select should allow you to enroll learners in your courses in both manual and automated ways that correlate with and support your administration and procedural activities.

- **Bulk Enrollment** – a bulk enrollment option is necessary, especially for organizations with hundreds or thousands of learners enrolling in their courses. Bulk enrollments or enrollments of multiple learners simultaneously are generally executed by importing a Comma-Separated Values (CSV) file into the LMS system. The CSV file is a standard file generated and exported by almost any organizational database system or from a simple Excel spreadsheet.

- **Manual Enrollment** – Manual enrollment allows an administrator to enroll one user at a time into a single course. Smaller education programs often use this option when an administrator would like to register a learner in a specific course outside of regular program start dates.

- **Self-Enrollment** – Most LMS platforms will allow organizations to give their learners the option to self-register for courses. This feature is typically used for education and training with corporate learners who are not paying tuition fees to access their courses. It provides them with the flexibility of being able to enroll in and access a course training program at a moment's notice. This allows employees greater control over their online training experiences.

Content Creation Tools

Course creation tools help educators and instructional designers create online course content (scripts, tests, quizzes, assessments, etc.). An easy-to-use content management system will save instructors time by making it easier to keep their courses up-to-date with new material. Look for an LMS that allows you to easily add content such as text, images, videos, audio files, or documents with just a few clicks. You should also be able to organize your content into folders or categories so that your students can quickly find what they are looking for. The primary function of an LMS should be that you can easily deliver course content to your learners, so it's essential to select an LMS that makes course creation as simple and straightforward as possible. A good LMS should let you drag, drop, and arrange content into place in multiple formats (PDFs, slides, videos, audio, learning objects, and even live training sessions).

The most widely used methods for standardizing learning content are SCORM and xAPI. SCORM is a set of technical standards for elearning materials. It provides the communication method and data models that permit the elearning content and LMS to work together. You will therefore want an LMS that can instantaneously upload SCORM and xAPI course files. Even if this sounds complicated or like something that you may not need to worry about right now if you are a smaller organization, it is a good idea to ensure your LMS has these features so that it can accommodate your content development needs as you grow.

Learner Profiles

Offering online education and training programs in your organization can provide a greater reach to learners from various backgrounds and geographies; however, this type of learning can also strip away the sense of personalization that occurs in face-to-face classroom interactions, making it difficult for learners and instructors to establish relationships. Your LMS should provide you with options to give your learners names, faces, and characteristics, which can help them relate to one another. An individual photo and short learner bio can bring a course to life, and when users can see and know one another, your virtual learning portal will begin to feel more like a community. We've all spent time in user environments where our profiles are represented by either a blank photo or an avatar, and it just doesn't create the same connection between learners.

Discussion Forums

A discussion forum is an asynchronous communication board where instructors and learners can read and post messages in their course. Discussions in a forum are organized into threads, where a user posts an original message to start a conversation. Then other users can post a response to it at any time. Discussion forums can be used for whole-class and smaller-group discussions and to provide areas of support and collaboration for learners.

Assessment Tools

A good LMS should have powerful assessment tools so instructors can easily create quizzes and tests for learners. Look for an LMS with options such as multiple-choice questions, matching questions, fill-in-the-blank questions, and drag-and-drop questions. You should also be able to set deadlines on assignments and track student progress over time.

Grade Book

Depending on the age of your learners, instructors will most likely require a grade book for assessments and evaluations. The grade book should be able to automatically record scores from assignments, quizzes, and other custom items that an instructor may add to the course. Learners should be able to immediately view any evaluations to keep track of their progress.

Collaboration Tools

Collaboration tools are essential in any modern learning environment. These tools are handy if instructors teach in a non-blended learning format, where direct contact with students is not possible. Look for an LMS with chat rooms, discussion boards, whiteboards, video conferencing capabilities, or other ways to encourage collaboration among students and teachers.

LMS Integrations

The LMS you select should help your organization automate some of the time-consuming administrative tasks that are part of managing your education and training program. Depending on your organizational size and the other technologies you are using, you may need your LMS to integrate seamlessly with your other systems. Typically, this means that whatever code is used to design your LMS will need to be compatible with the code you are using for your website, user database management, or accounting systems. You will then be able to automate actions such as user creation and course access, data synchronization, enrollments, marks reporting, and more.

Storage Requirements

You will also want to know what storage capacity is required to run and maintain your LMS. Will users be able to upload assignments, and if so, will there be any size restrictions? Are there any file type limitations to what data the system can store? Typically, the greater the number of users accessing your learning system, the larger the amount of online storage/server space you will require for hosting your data. If you are an accredited education and training program, you will also need to consider how long you are required to retain learner data for inspection authorities.

Automated Notifications and Alerts

Any LMS you select should be able to provide automated alerts to instructors and students so they are aware of any new communications, announcements, or evaluations available in their course. The system should also provide alerts to administrators on system updates or any potential issues occurring that they will need to manage.

Mobile Learning (M-Learning) Ready

Mobile learning or m-learning refers to users accessing education and training content through mobile devices. In today's world, we use our smartphones and tablets for everything. In many areas of the world, families may not have a home computer, but almost everyone, rich or poor, will have access to some type of mobile device. People can now learn whenever and from wherever they want as long as their mobile device has access to the Internet. Thus, your LMS must support multiple formats of content and be compatible with a variety of mobile device types. You'll want to know if a mobile app for your LMS is available through either Apple or Google Play.

In my experience, we cannot take for granted that an LMS and its features will easily function on the most popular mobile devices. I have known organizations to develop beautiful learning portals but then negate the testing phase of launching the materials on various Internet browsers and mobile devices. Unfortunately, they typically discover a myriad of glitchy technological issues as users from multiple devices begin to engage with the digital learning content. The most common problems seem to be with the display of images and functionality of tests and quizzes. Unless you are a corporation that mandates the exact technology your employees must use to access your online training materials (and can therefore limit any testing to solely that one technology), it is crucial to ensure that your LMS system and apps are compatible with a broad range of mobile device types and Internet browsers.

Ensuring that mobile learning is available to your users is a great way to ensure that learners can conveniently take any required education and training materials with them to access from anywhere and at any time. This is especially important if learning occurs outside of regular work hours. A mobile learning option also lets users receive real-time feedback and notifications from their instructor and course, thereby increasing their motivation to participate and learn.

Learner Analytics

Learning analytics are the measurement, collection, and analysis of data generated by learners in your courses. Analytics are used to gauge the effectiveness of the learning program you are offering and to help determine the criteria that will predict learner success. Learning analytics from your LMS will provide data on how often your learners access their course, their navigation and learning patterns, and valuable information that can help you troubleshoot any causes for course attrition rates. Some types of learning analytics which you will want to extract from your LMS include:

1. **Completion Rates** – what percentage of your learners are completing their elearning course? How long does it take them to progress through and complete each task or learning module? Are there specific learning activities that almost all users take too long to complete? This information can give you valuable feedback on any changes or updates you should make to your courses. If the majority of your learners are not completing your elearning courses, you may need to reevaluate your elearning strategy. Conversely, if most learners are breezing through a course and achieving 100% on all tasks, then perhaps it's time to make some elements of your course more challenging.

2. **Portal Access Data** – what time of day are most instructors and learners accessing and using your system? Are your users located in the same time zone as your organization? This knowledge can assist you in designing learner support staff scheduling and instructor office hours and provide you with advance preparation for high-traffic times on your learning website. It can also

provide data on the types of systems and devices learners use to access your online education program.

3. **Online Learner Surveys** – surveys are one of the most direct and measurable forms of feedback you can receive from your learners, as they allow them to share their honest opinions and recommendations. We can also use surveys and polls for group and classroom evaluations between learners. Are your learners connecting with your program, or are they finding the activities and systems difficult to navigate?

Conclusion

This general overview of the most popular LMS options and features can help guide you on your journey as you consider whether your organization can benefit from acquiring and launching an LMS. Knowing what's available and your options can help you as a leader ask the right questions to determine which LMS is the best fit for your organization and learners' needs.

Leadership Questions

1. What types of features are essential to your organization when selecting an LMS?

2. In what ways does your LMS need to be able to support your distance education and training goals?

3. What do you feel is the most important information which should appear in your organization's LMS dashboard for instructors and learners?

4. Will your organization enroll your LMS users manually or import them in bulk from another system?

5. What types of user analytics and data should your LMS be able to collect and store for your organization?

LMS Design Theme Considerations

We all know that first impressions are important. This applies to LMS design just as much as it does in the physical world. If you're a leader in an organization that offers online courses, you know how important it is to have an LMS design theme that is both aesthetically pleasing and technologically effective. Your LMS is often the first point of contact between your instructors and learners. A good LMS design theme tells learners a lot about the education and training program you will offer them and the level of professionalism they can expect while completing your program.

An interesting LMS theme and interface will create a seamless user experience, enhancing learner engagement and making your virtual learning system easy and comfortable for instructors and learners to use. Let's take a closer look at why having a good LMS theme is so important.

Boosts Learner Engagement

The goal of any virtual learning world should be to attract and engage learners. If your LMS design theme isn't appealing to the eye, chances are learners will not complete their courses with you or enroll in further studies in your program. Worse, they will be unlikely to refer your education and training program to their friends and colleagues. That's why it's essential to have an aesthetically pleasing and easy-to-use LMS design theme that encourages learner engagement. Users are more likely to complete their courses if they can easily navigate your online environment without feeling overwhelmed or confused. An aesthetically pleasing LMS also increases the chances of them giving your program a 5-star review.

Sets You Apart From Other Programs

Having a great LMS design theme can help you stand out from other similar programs in your industry. If two universities, colleges, or business organizations offer the same diploma or certification program, but one has an attractive, well-designed virtual world while the other has a poorly designed one, chances are both instructors and learners will opt to be part of the better-looking site. So it's important to choose a good LMS design theme that sets you apart from other programs.

Establishes Brand Identity & Trustworthiness

A good website design theme can help establish brand identity and trustworthiness with potential instructors and learners. When people visit your virtual learning world, they form an opinion about who you are and the quality of the education and training program you offer based on how everything looks and feels. This includes colors, fonts, images, layout, etc.

If they like what they see, they'll be more likely to trust that you're offering a valuable and quality learning program that will meet their needs. If, on the other hand, they don't like what they see, they may immediately withdraw from a course and not stay to find out what valuable learning experiences you have to offer them.

Essential LMS Design Theme Components

But what are the essential components of a good LMS design theme for your distance education and training program? In this section, we'll look at the necessary items you will want to consider in your LMS design theme and its overall design blueprint. If you have an existing LMS system and are planning to redesign and update it, this section can help you determine what existing items you may wish to update over time to improve or enhance the look and feel of your virtual learning portal.

1. Interface

The User Interface of your LMS is how the learner interacts with the system. Icons, buttons, menus, search bars, welcome screens, and news feeds are just a few examples of the components that make up the user interface in your LMS. A learner's interactions with the system interface should be straightforward so as not to become a barrier to engaging with the learning activities.

Interface Checklist

A user interface should therefore be simple, attractive, and intuitive and should incorporate the following features:

- **Minimal Scrolling** – there should be minimal scrolling in your content design. Most people dislike pages and pages of scrolling to read and access information. When it comes to instructions, few will read them if they fall outside of the main viewing screen (studies show very few people scroll to read instructions);

- **AODA/WAGG** compliance – your LMS should provide the ability for captions and text alternatives for images and multimedia;

- **Adequate Whitespace** is incorporated into the overall design;

- **Use the Chunking Principle** – keep action item-type instructions and "to-do lists" to 5 or fewer items (chunking principle);

- **Simple Media is Used** – sound and animations should not compete with text;

- **Large and Clear Fonts are Used** – ensure the use of large, clear fonts within your site and in emails;

- **No Time Limits** – avoid time limits when asking learners to provide a response or information;

- **Avoid Blinking Images** – people with photosensitive epilepsy may have seizures triggered by displays that flicker, flash, or blink. This is particularly the case if the flash has a high intensity and is within certain frequency ranges;

- **Maintain a Consistent Color Theme** – a consistent color theme should be used to define similar functions in your LMS. Themes should be simple throughout the site and in any system-generated emails or notifications.

2. Whitespace

Whitespace is one of the most overlooked and underutilized elements contributing to an impressive layout in your LMS platform design. Too often, whitespace is viewed as empty or underutilized space and, therefore, a waste of computer screen real estate. However, ensuring adequate whitespace is one of the most fundamental parts of a good learning portal design.

When instructional designers talk about whitespace, they actually mean negative space. This is the portion of a webpage left unmarked in the space between graphics, columns, and margins. Whitespace in your LMS design provides visual breathing room for the eyes of users. Providing adequate whitespace ensures that your LMS layout is easy on the eyes and makes learners want to keep reading.

Below are some of the benefits of incorporating sufficient whitespace into your LMS design:

- **An Increase in Content Legibility:** When learners navigate your LMS, they should be able to see where they are going and easily digest the content they are reading. Whitespace between paragraphs and around blocks of text and images helps people understand what they are reading and adds to a better learners' experience overall.

- **Increased Focus & Decreased Distractions:** Today, most learners are bombarded by information overload and a myriad of advertisements and distracting information when browsing websites. A good amount of whitespace can increase learner focus by limiting the unnecessary distractions that slow them down when navigating your LMS. Even a slight padding of whitespace around objects will help to draw attention to specific and essential areas of your learning portal.

- **Professional Look and Feel:** Your learning portal's first impression after users log in matters greatly. The key is to balance your designs and let whitespace act as a great tool to separate chunks of content for easy accessibility and improved user experience. Solid layouts and suitable/simple color schemes with whitespace used in the correct manner will add a sense of professional elegance to your LMS portal.

Whitespace not only creates harmony and balance in your LMS design, it can also lead a reader from one element to another. Your primary goals should be to make your learning portal look simple and uncluttered and to deliver your education and training information to your learners in an easily accessible way.

3. Navigation

Online learners must be able to easily access the information and tools they need in your learning portal. Figuring out how to move from one page to the next should not involve a steep learning curve. Confusing and cluttered elearning navigation controls can often be a roadblock for online learners. For this reason, it's best to use familiar navigation controls in your learning portal and avoid avant-garde icon innovations that learners are likely to find confusing. It's best to keep LMS navigation controls simple, thus ensuring that your online learners can get through their elearning course with minimal stress.

Navigation Checklist

Here are some best practices to consider when designing your LMS site navigation:

- Site functions should have predictable and consistent locations;

- learners should be able to easily identify where they are in your virtual learning site;

- learners can easily navigate to a location on the site using breadcrumbs (in addition to the side menus);

- links have specific names to help learners find and navigate education and training content;

- icons or small visuals are used to define functions. Most of the population has a strong visual learning preference. Visual icons can help learners become easily familiar and comfortable with the how/what/where functions of your website. For example, when we see a print button, we all know we can press it to print an item no matter where we are on a site (transitional knowledge). You may wish to have an icon to indicate a "to-do" area in online courses, and if you add discussion forums, you should have an icon representing a place to chat/message.

4. Technology

A published elearning course in your LMS isn't much different from a website. All the course content sits in a folder on a server (think giant tech filing cabinet with all of your course files in it). Most technological considerations are already built into your LMS; however, below are a few important features and options you should be on the lookout for regarding technical considerations when your tech staff begins configuring your learning portal settings.

Technology Checklist

- Content can be presented using assistive technologies (such as screen readers) without losing its meaning;

- all content can be published from the LMS using one of the standard protocols, for example, SCORM, AICC, or xAPI;

- learning portal and apps work reliably for the current main browsers and mobile devices; have been tested with mobile apps for both Apple and Android;

- site is compatible with both Mac and PC;

- avoid using CAPTCHAs (learner challenges involving distorted letter forms) and give learners enough time to read and use content;

- the LMS helps learners avoid and correct mistakes by making error messages specific;

- geography & Internet Speed–slow DSL connections may still be the only Internet option for many rural areas; this should be kept in mind when developing graphics/videos. Consider providing high bandwidth media as an "extra" vs. as a key component for lessons.

Testing your Design Theme

When selecting an effective LMS design theme, there are a couple of essential components you need to test run to ensure success. Organizations will run two primary tests to ensure the LMS design theme is an intuitive system that looks great and functions properly, thus creating an excellent experience for their users.

1. Usability Testing
Usability testing is a vital element of successful LMS design themes. Usability testing involves assessing the user experience by having actual users interact with your LMS to identify any issues or areas for improvement. This type of testing helps identify potential problems before they become significant issues, allowing you to make improvements more quickly and efficiently. Often, organizations will assign a beta group of users to test a new theme before formally launching it.

2. Mobile Responsiveness
A mobile-responsive LMS design theme is essential in today's world, where more people use mobile devices than ever before. In some countries, learners will access virtual worlds using only their mobile devices. Your theme should be optimized for mobile devices so learners can access content from anywhere and at any time. Mobile-responsive themes help ensure that learners have a consistent experience across

all devices, which can help improve instructor and learner engagement with the courses offered by your organization.

Conclusion

A successful and appealing LMS design theme is crucial for distance education and training programs. Not only does it need to look good, but it also needs to be user-friendly and easy to navigate. An effective design will create a seamless experience for instructors and learners, fostering engagement and making learning more enjoyable.

Employing usability testing before launching a new LMS design theme can help identify potential problems before they become big issues; mobile responsiveness testing ensures that learners have a consistent experience regardless of what device they're using to access your courses. Keeping these considerations in mind can help create a robust learning environment for your organization.

Leadership Questions

1. What are the goals of the LMS design theme for your distance education and training program?

2. What features can make your LMS design theme both aesthetically pleasing and effective?

3. How can you use your LMS design theme to attract and engage learners?

4. How important are branding and aesthetics in your LMS design theme?

5. How can you tell if your LMS design theme has adequate navigation controls for instructors and users?

Common LMS Price Models

When selecting a learning management system (LMS), countless options are available. But how do you know which one is right for your organization? One of the most important factors to consider is the pricing model and structure of the LMS you're considering. The initial set-up costs and ongoing maintenance fees will probably be top-level considerations when you are evaluating LMS options for your organization. Besides being able to meet your education and training needs, any LMS system must have a pricing structure that aligns with your organization's fiscal requirements. Here are some standard LMS pricing models that will give you an idea of what you can ask for.

Pay per User Model

This fee structure is usually available for cloud-based LMS systems and involves paying for each person using the LMS. In this scenario, the LMS provider controls, hosts, and maintains the LMS platform. As a result, your organization will not have to devote as many resources to maintaining the LMS; however, this also often means that you will have less control over customizing the overall look and feel, as well as features available to you for your users.

Pay-As-You-Go Model

Similar to the prepaid phone concept, the 'pay-as-you-go' model is exactly what it sounds like—you pay for the amount of time you spend using the system. Organizations in this model are charged an hourly or per-use fee, depending on the features they select and their usage levels. This model works well for organizations that have fluctuating learner numbers or require access to certain features only occasionally.

Subscription Model

The subscription model differs from the 'pay-as-you-go' model in that it offers users unlimited access to all features within the LMS according to the agreed-upon terms and conditions. They usually offer annual or monthly subscriptions and discounts for longer-term commitments. This allows your organization an unlimited number of users; however, the hosting fees for the LMS will be much higher.

Your monthly fee depends on the features and upgrades you select for your organization. In this model, the LMS often comes with a package selection containing predetermined features. This works well for organizations that need consistent access to an LMS over an extended period, especially if you don't want to worry about paying extra fees when usage increases beyond what was initially planned.

The License Model

The license model is like the subscription model because it provides organizations with unlimited access. However, there is one key difference: Users own their license outright after purchasing it from the vendor. Depending on the LMS vendor, licenses are offered on a one-time or annual basis, with discounts typically given if multiple licenses are purchased simultaneously. This is a great option for organizations looking for long-term ownership of their LMS.

You will, however, have to pay for any upgrades or updates to the LMS, similar to when you purchase other software packages for your organization, such as Microsoft Office or Adobe, and a new version comes out. You also have to pay for and organize any hosting required by the LMS or outsource it to an LMS hosting company.

Free Open-Source LMS Solutions

There are some fantastic free, open-source alternatives to paid LMS solutions. However, the setup and maintenance will require you to have an in-house technology person or outsource this role to another technology company. Open-source software projects/products are initiatives created through open exchange and collaborative participation designed to benefit communities. Programmers who have access to a computer program's source code can improve it by adding features or fixing parts that don't always work correctly. The program authors then make the source code available to others who want to view it, copy it, learn from it, alter it, use it, or share it. An open-source LMS is an excellent option for organizations that already have in-house elearning tech staff with coding expertise. It also works for those willing to invest in some online training time to bring over tech people currently filling other roles in the organization.

Many organizations prefer open-source software because they can fully control the look and feel of it and the features that are used, along with the costs that are associated with it. You can incorporate your branding, adjust the layout, and personalize your learner dashboards without copyright or licensing restrictions.

It can also be considered more secure and stable than proprietary software, as programmers can spot errors or omissions in the program that a vendor company might have missed. When a code is open-source and available for public viewing, there can be no private collection of information or data that users or organizations are unaware of.

To access an open-source solution, any user can download the software free of charge. There are also some alternate open-source platform options known as freemium systems. In this type of LMS, you can get the basic system code for free but must pay a nominal fee for additional upgrades or add-ons. This is an excellent choice for organizations that cannot afford monthly or yearly licensing fees.

Many open-source LMS platforms also have an online user community where you can find tips, tricks, and advice to help you master the LMS platform and its features. Your tech staff can also post questions when troubleshooting an LMS issue, share pointers, and collaborate with other learning organizations. The key is to find a system with an active user community and online support resources.

The biggest drawback to using an open-source LMS is that you are unlikely to have access to any dedicated live or email tech support if you need it. This means it can be difficult to rapidly solve some tech issues you may encounter, which can be a significant issue for organizations that would like advanced support services. If you encounter any problems, you must rely solely on your in-house tech team and the online support community.

Our Move to an Open-Sourced LMS

When our organization made the move to an open-source LMS, we selected Moodle, and we had a great experience with it. We could customize the look and feel of it for our school and easily modify and set up a custom-themed look for partner organizations working with us. Initially, we had a great school tech already on staff managing our school website and e-commerce systems to set up and install our LMS for us. As we grew into using some of the more advanced features and functionalities of the LMS system, we then outsourced single-task advanced installations to a provider.

So, for example, if we wanted to add a custom LMS feature to work with our existing system, we would outsource the job to a specialty tech company on a one-time basis.

Understanding Learning Management Systems

We created an outline of what we wanted our Moodle system to do and then obtained a quotation from providers to develop and add this new feature. I liked this model for building our system, as it allowed us to restrict and control the cost of any fresh additions to our Moodle distance learning system on an as-we-needed-it (and could afford it) basis. Using this strategy allowed us to grow and build without requiring us to commit to long-term expenditures with an outsourced provider.

At one point, we encountered a technical glitch/error that our local staff could not solve. We again successfully used the same outsourcing model to solve the issue by reaching out to a company specializing in Moodle. They solved the problem for us for a fee within 24 hours. We also did some advance research on the ease of availability of support providers for a Moodle system. If your organization goes this route, choosing an open-source LMS with an extensive knowledge base is important.

I am a big fan of Moodle and have used it when setting up elearning projects with both smaller and larger organizations. One limitation we did, however, repeatedly encounter when attempting to customize our system was when a new update or version of Moodle came out. Installing a new version of Moodle would overwrite any specialized customizations we had built. These would then have to be re-added by our tech team—not a big deal for minor customizations, but definitely something you will want to keep in mind when you are considering customizations and planning LMS updates.

Conclusion

Investing in an LMS typically represents a long-term commitment for your distance education and training program. Knowing which LMS pricing models work best for your organization can help you make an informed decision when selecting an LMS provider. Pay-as-you-go, subscription, license, and open-source models each offer unique advantages depending on your organizational needs. So it's best to take your time to explore which one will work best for you. Whichever option you choose, be sure to evaluate all of your options against both your short-term and long-term budget requirements.

Leadership Questions

1. What are your top considerations when choosing to invest in an LMS?

2. What pricing model do you feel would best align with the resources and needs of your distance education and training program?

3. Will your organization consider a paid LMS pricing model, or do you have the in-house resources to manage an open-source model?

Creating Your Elearning Test Environment

One of the most important lessons I learned in managing an international distance education program was the importance of having an elearning test environment. A test environment is a learning portal that is an exact duplicate of your virtual world. Its purpose is to allow your technology people to make changes to your virtual world and test the results without impacting your organization's employees and learners. It is essentially a non-live online learning playground where you can try things out and make system and visual changes before launching them in your real virtual world, which is live with your users working away on their courses.

It Doesn't Always Pay to be First

Every one of us has had that moment when we log in to our computers or mobile phones and receive an alert that says, "update available." And typically, we all have similar reactions to this notice. Should we click update right away and go for it to see what's new and possibly awesome on our device? Or should we put the update off as long as possible until we can no longer stand seeing the notification in our list (let's see what happens to everyone else first)?

And there's a very good reason for this range of our reactions. Many years ago, early in my career, I would have slotted myself into the early adopter category. When a new update or innovation came out for my devices, I wanted to explore it immediately. But after many instances of clicking that update button the moment I saw it, I also quickly learned that in the world of technology, there are almost always minor consequences to being first. Unfortunately, after a massive program update, it is not uncommon to experience technology gremlins, such as phone alerts that have stopped working or a computer that will no longer boot up. You lose hours and sometimes days or weeks of frustrating work time trying to troubleshoot what has happened. It often feels like falling into a technological rabbit hole. I had an incident after installing a Google phone update the first day it was released; the microphone for my language learning app learning (which I use every day) stopped working. It took six weeks before the developer solved the problem, and I got my microphone back.

Fast-forward a few years, and wow, have I learned! Now when an update notification magically appears on my phone or computer, my mind instead reminds me… don't do it… don't hit the button… you don't have time for what may happen. Let everyone else try this out first, and then by the time you join the masses, hopefully, most of any bugs that may occur will be resolved.

Why Should You Have a Test Environment for Online Courses?

So all of this leads me back to the importance of having an elearning test environment for your distance education and training program. One of the most significant advantages of having a duplicate learning portal is that it makes testing much easier. Instead of trying to guess what might happen when you implement changes or launch new initiatives, you can set up the entire process on a duplicate learning portal. This will allow you to see exactly how everything works in real time without any risk. This allows your organization to troubleshoot and fine-tune your processes before making any major changes.

When you have live users in your virtual learning portal, you want to avoid experimentation, making changes, or running an update while users navigate and interact with your system. Your tech people might tell you that the change will not affect users, but this will probably be true only 50% of the time. When it comes to massive learning portal updates, providers will tell you the update is ready to go for your virtual world and that they have tested everything out and it's going to run fine. All I can say is that in my 20-year career working with LMS systems and virtual learning worlds, major updates went 100% smoothly without a glitch exactly 0 times. It did not matter if we were using one of the largest and best providers available in our area or our own tech team on a smaller system; there were *always* glitches to work out. If you're lucky, they are smaller errors that can be resolved quickly. Still, I've seen instances with updates resulting in massive faults where the images in every course disappeared, tests stopped functioning, along with a myriad of other things that can happen. If you are still a small organization, when this happens with under 50 students enrolled in your program, it's not good, but not the end of the world. If you are a larger education and training organization with thousands of students accessing your courses and this happens, then you need to get ready for your phone lines to light up.

Having a duplicate test learning portal helps your organization save time and money because you don't have to spend time troubleshooting issues in your live learning environment. Additionally, since errors can be identified quickly in the duplicate learning portal, your organization won't waste time dealing with customer service issues or lost revenue from mistakes made in your live environment.

An LMS Provider's Test Portal vs. Your LMS Portal

Why do updates seem to run smoothly when LMS tech providers test things in their virtual learning portal but then go wonky when they are applied to your virtual world? The primary variable is that your learning portal is not an empty shell containing only the newest updated system information; it is loaded with content for your courses. The materials and media objects may have been grandfathered into some of these courses over time. It can be challenging for LMS tech companies to anticipate how their system will deal with content developed using technology from a few years ago. So the best solution is always to conduct a test of any proposed updates or changes in your own test environment. Since it is a duplicate learning portal to the one you operate in, it is more likely to react and behave the way your live portal will after applying an update.

When we conducted updates in our own elearning world test environment, even after the provider announced everything transitioned perfectly, I would *still* send in my team of staff and ask each person to dedicate a few hours in a specific course to click on learning content items, take a quiz, and interact with the newly updated online space. They were to imitate the roles of students and teachers to see if they encountered any unusual behavior in the system. Once we were confident that any potential issues were resolved, then and only then did we launch updates on the live system (notifying users in advance that this would occur).

Conclusion

An elearning test environment that duplicates your existing virtual world offers many benefits that can help your organization save time and money. It also ensures major changes to your environment do not disrupt the progress and experience of your learners. Whether you are launching a new LMS initiative or making changes to your existing LMS, investing in a duplicate platform is a very low-cost way to ensure that everything goes smoothly without any surprises.

Leadership Questions

1. Do you have an elearning test environment where your instructors, technology staff, and providers can launch big and small updates or proposed changes to your environment?

2. What policies should your organization have regarding testing and launching new technologies?

LMS Security & Privacy

Your virtual education and training world, especially in the corporate training sector, will contain sensitive information about your learners and employees that you will absolutely want to keep safe. That's why ensuring that your online learning portal is secure from threats such as website hijacking, website spoofing, and other cyber threats is important.

To combat cyber threats, organizations must first understand what vulnerabilities their system may have. Cyber incidents can be embarrassing and impact your organization's image and the confidence and loyalty of your clients. Most people think of tech security for their organization as an IT issue, but it is also a critical brand issue.

The first step in securing your online learning portal is having clear security measures in place. You don't need to be a technology specialist to comprehend some of the security issues your program may face; you just need to be able to ask the right questions of both your tech employees and any outside technological providers you may be using. Below are some of the most common delicate spots you may wish to consider for review.

Website Hijacking

In my career as the director of an international distance education program, we had multiple instances of attempted hacking and spoofing of both our website and our online

LMS. Since we were one of the few fully online accredited high school programs in Ontario, Canada, offering our program globally, it seems we were also what some security organizations would call a value target.

In our early years of operation, our school webpage server was hijacked and replaced with a foreign special interest group page. We were such a small organization when this happened, with less than 100 students per year attending our program, that we were wholly unprepared for this occurrence.

A website browser hijacker is a malware program that modifies your web browser settings without your permission and redirects the users to other websites. It is often called a browser redirect virus because it redirects the browser to other, usually malicious, websites. Such an occurrence may result in a hijacking event that damages your brand and impacts your users. Thus, it is crucial to have a conversation with your tech team and hosting provider for both your website and LMS to find out what security measures they have in place to help prevent code injections into your website.

Congratulations, You've Been Spoofed

Website spoofing is a scam where cyber criminals create a website closely resembling a trusted brand and a domain virtually identical to a brand's web domain. Website spoofing aims to lure potential clients, suppliers, partners, and employees to a fraudulent website. Once there, it attempts

Understanding Learning Management Systems

to convince them to share sensitive information such as login credentials, Social Security numbers, credit card information, or bank account numbers.

After a decade of operations, just when I thought I'd seen it all and our organization felt better versed in anticipating potential security threats that could be encountered in our school's virtual world, a counterfeit organization in Korea completely spoofed our entire school website. They copied every single website page and then set them up in an alternate domain. The website domain they purchased was very close to our own (I think it had only one letter that was different). They then began fraudulently representing themselves as our legitimate school through their new site. Since we were oblivious to this occurrence (how would you know someone is impersonating you in Korea), our days and functions continued as usual, and we were none the wiser.

The day we received a phone call from our Ministry of Education inspector asking when we had expanded into Korea was the day that we, as an organization, had to reconsider security entirely. Although we were now an international school with thousands of students accessing our program every year, I could not fathom how we were valuable enough for foreign organizations to target us in this fashion. It was both a ginormous headache and a compliment to our international success at the same time. Because of the Korea incident, we purchased upwards of 25 website domain names closest to the one used by our organization. At about $15 per domain name per year, this totaled about $375 per year. The cost of being impersonated and trying to have law enforcement in another country take down a fraudulent website spoofing your organization is incalculable.

Blocking Foreign IP Addresses

As an additional measure to the website spoofing incident, we also then blocked all IP addresses coming from any countries where our learners did not live.

Many education and training systems seeking to grow do not consider limiting some areas of the world where users can access their LMS system from. Our initial thoughts are always that we want to be able to grow and accept new learners from anywhere worldwide. The fact is, however, there are some countries where the hijacking of your distance learning portal, the hacking of your administrator and teacher email addresses, and just general spoofing of your organization's identity are more likely to happen. And these are also countries you are very unlikely to receive new learners from or do business with. For example, if you offer an online education program delivered in English, it is unlikely that learners from countries whose first or second language is not English will become your clients.

In today's world, 15 years later, there are entirely new challenges to doing this. Those who wish to access your virtual world for illegitimate reasons often use technology such as VPNs. Websites like PayPal and Amazon are now blocking VPN access from known providers for this reason. It can be a controversial topic, as some users will also state they are using a VPN for security. This is a discussion you will need to have with your LMS host and security provider so that you can make your own decision about what is best for your organization.

In my view, one of the major challenges in offering fully online distance education programs today is user misrepresentation and fraud. Even your learner analytics depend on being able to obtain accurate data from your system users. The credibility and integrity of your program depend upon transparent, accurate, and legitimate learner results in your education and training program, thus justifying any enhanced security measures you deem necessary.

Creating Multi-Level of User Roles

User roles in your LMS are vital, as they provide each user with appropriate access rights and privileges to your system. You will want to ensure that the LMS you select for your organization allows you to create multiple user roles with permission levels corresponding to each role. An LMS that will allow your tech people to create custom user roles where you determine each role's permissions is even better. Examples of standard user roles organizations use with their LMS are as follows:

- **Developer** – this role typically has all permissions available and can access and change the code in your LMS.

- **Administrator** – this role usually has permission to access your LMS site data, enroll users, and view all classrooms in your virtual world. This user role cannot, however, modify your LMS system code.

- **Teacher/Instructor** – this user role can upload content into specified classrooms in your LMS. They can post lessons and announcements and access their own students' information and grade book data. This user role cannot view information for students in other courses and cannot change the LMS system code.

- **Student/Learner** – this user role can view and interact with content in their assigned online classroom. This user can typically communicate with other learners but cannot modify other users' data or learning content in the course.

You can also define many other user roles in your LMS, and it's up to your team to determine what types of permissions should be assigned to specific roles, depending on the functions that need to be performed. Consideration must be given to your organization's privacy policies regarding access to user data.

The Human Element

Anti-virus software, firewalls, and data encryption are considered go-to security solutions for most organizations. Each measure is designed to stop cyber criminals from accessing your systems. Unfortunately, they have little impact on an organization's most common security vulnerability—human error.

We once had an instructor for several of our courses who had saved her password to access her virtual classroom in her personal Hotmail account. Her Hotmail account was subsequently hacked, and seven of her online courses were deleted. This was devastating to her and resulted in overtime for our entire team as we invested almost two weeks of hours restoring her courses from backup (a system backup in 2004 was not what it is today).

Employees working remotely from home for a portion of their weekly hours have been on the rise for years, but the global COVID-19 pandemic has catapulted this practice into the next era. While having staff such as instructors in your distance education program working from home yields many benefits, it may also come with substantial drawbacks. Studies repeatedly show an organization is more likely to be breached because of an employee misplacing or being tricked into handing over sensitive information than by a criminal breaking into its online systems. Employees working from a home office use home Internet connections rather than the securer ones IT professionals install in your organization's offices. Less secure home networks can open up every device in an employee's house to become a target for cyber threats.

Other unintended actions can create vulnerabilities as well. For example, instructors with family or guests in the house may log into your student database or LMS from home to access student information and coursework. If they leave their computer to make a coffee with their screen still logged in, everyone in the house can see/possibly access a learner's private data. As an organization, it's challenging to stop these types of things from happening when an employee is working from home, but you can institute some measures to help prevent breaches. Some examples include:

- **Staff Awareness Training** – this is critical to reducing the risk of employee error, especially when instructors and assistants work from their home computer systems. Staff awareness training is part of a comprehensive set of best practices an organization should follow, whereby routine measures are established to minimize security vulnerabilities and user data breaches.

- **Encryption** – ensure all instructor and learner data are encrypted and stored securely. In addition, make sure that access to the portal is limited only to those who have permission or are authorized by your organization.

- **User Timeouts** – user logins to your systems should be set to timeout after a short period of user inactivity. This is important so that screens with confidential data cannot be unintentionally left open or logged into when working from a home office.

- **Classifying Levels of Data Sensitivity** – many organizations limit the types of data or records accessible from home. I know of one education organization that works with instructors in a segregated access format whereby instructors can access student courses from home. However, if they need access to more sensitive student information, for example, a learner's medical information—they must come into the office/school. Organizations should determine what data types need to be protected and create a Data Classification Policy to classify data based on sensitivity.

- **Strong Password Requirements** – when someone wants to access your virtual learning portal, they should always have to log into it using a unique username and password combination. Did you know that brute force hacking software can find a single dictionary word password within one second? Fluffy passwords should not be allowed; the minimum password requirement should be the uppercase, lowercase, letter, number, and symbol combination. It's important to make sure it's highly complicated to steal a learner's credentials. Getting access to your platform should be just the first step. You will want to make sure each user logging in to your virtual world is exactly whom they claim to be and that they didn't steal someone else's credentials.

- **Two-Step Authentication** – many platforms are now adding security features requiring two-step authentication when users access their course from a new device or an unusual out-of-country location. Currently, two-step authentication is one of the easiest deterrents to unauthorized access to distance learning systems.

Where to Store Learner Data?

There are now many laws that organizations must adhere to regarding how they store and manage digital user data. This includes heightened requirements when an organization is storing personal learner data, especially for those considered minors (usually under the age of eighteen or nineteen). Specific laws for your province, state, or country will vary greatly; thus, if you're storing any user data, it is wise to invest in a legal consultation with an expert. You will want someone who is up-to-date on current laws and can help create your organization's privacy policy and technological data storage requirements. This may seem like an unnecessary expenditure; however, it will ensure you are protecting your users and doing things right from the beginning. It will also help you avoid problems and issues down the road should your system ever be breached.

My organization's strategy for storing learner data was as follows:

1. If You Don't Need it, Don't Store it

If specific personal data is not required for operational or legal reporting purposes to education authorities, then it should not be stored. If you don't have the information in the first place, it can't be stolen from you if your system is breached. This also includes credit card information for users. If you're a smaller organization with limited technological capabilities, you can have a third-party payment provider process all of your user payments. Some examples might be your bank's merchant system or other systems such as PayPal, Shopify, Square, etc. These systems connect directly to your website; however, all responsibility and liability for client credit card information shifts to the payment organization designed and built security-wise to collect payments.

2. Separate Databases for Sensitive Data

We stored very little learner data on the published website of the LMS system. Only the basics, such as a user's first name and maybe the last name, were held there. We stored all other pertinent data required for government reporting in a separate, highly secured, non-published database to which only administrators and instructors (with limited permissions) had access. If you're marketing your elearning program and its website, the attached database is not the place to store your most sensitive data. Institutions should also consider keeping html lessons on a separate server from their learning portal (a server location that is not advertised publicly). Moodle, for example, can point to content stored outside the LMS, and the lesson still opens in Moodle as if it were created there. This ensures that as you grow if there is an automated brute force attack on your Moodle site, your content is safely secured and stored in a separate server location. It sounds complicated, but it is actually pretty simple to set up.

3. Geographic Server Locations

We ensured the servers used to store our LMS user data were located in a North American country. Is the storage of your data outsourced to any other country? If you are using an LMS provider, this is a question you will definitely want to ask them. Many providers hosting your data for you will outsource the storage to foreign countries which offer these services at a very low cost. Unfortunately, many of these countries also have questionable security policies and protocols. If you are using an open-sourced LMS and your tech people purchase server space on a host such as Amazon, this is again a question you will want to ask them. Do the web servers have firewalls and antivirus software installed? Has a method for generating regular automated backups of your online learning portal been established?

4. Using Firewalls

Finally, don't forget about security measures such as firewalls and antivirus software. Firewalls help protect your systems from malicious attacks, while antivirus software can detect and remove any malware before it gets into your system. These measures will go a long way toward keeping your online learning portal safe from any outside interference or data theft attempts.

Most organizations will, unfortunately, experience at least one of the cybercrime incidents described in this section as their learner numbers grow. It's vital that any LMS or website hosting provider you are using (or your own tech team) takes potential threats seriously and is able to describe to you how they are preparing in advance to combat and head off any possible threats.

Conclusion

Security should always be top of mind when launching and maintaining a virtual distance education and training program, especially when storing sensitive instructor or learner information. By taking the necessary steps outlined in this section and those recommended by your tech team, you can help protect yourself against potential cyber threats that could otherwise jeopardize your organization's data safety and established brand.

Leadership Questions

1. What security measures do you currently have in place to prevent cyber threats and protect learner data at your organization?

2. What additional security protocols could you add to further protect yourself?

5

REGULATORY LANDSCAPES & ACADEMIC FRAUD

ELEARNING GOLD—ANNETTE LEVESQUE

Managing Relationships With Regulatory Authorities

The world of virtual education and training is constantly changing. As technology advances, so must the strategies used to deliver that education. But while new strategies may be necessary to stay ahead of the curve, they can also bring with them several obstacles, including regulatory program inspectors. So how do you navigate these inspectors while also having the freedom you need to innovate?

Program inspectors are individuals or entities responsible for ensuring educational institutions comply with all applicable regulations. They are typically hired by regulatory bodies, such as government agencies, accrediting bodies, or professional organizations. Program inspectors conduct regular on-site visits to review programs and ensure they meet specific standards.

As an organization delivering virtual education and training, one of the major challenges in offering a program online that will lead to a degree, certificate, or licensing for a specific profession is that you will probably have a governing body that provides oversight for the accreditation of your program. Whether your courses will lead to a high school diploma, university degree, or electrician's license, the success criteria and curriculum will be impacted by regulatory authorities outside your organization.

Making changes to the education and training program you offer to meet any new curriculum requirements is very different in a virtual world than in a face-to-face classroom. The development of your elearning courses can be a costly venture involving much time and hard work on behalf of your team. Substituting, redeveloping, or executing major updates in a virtual world will take time and planning. Hopefully, you are governed by an authority that has adapted its education and training policies to provide you with adequate time to institute these changes; however, this often will not be the case.

I remember in our early years, when the Ministry of Education would issue a mandatory curriculum change, they expected teachers and schools to teach the new curriculum often within only a month of receiving the notice. Teachers in face-to-face classrooms were constantly upset by this. It gave them little time to prepare, and no new textbooks or resources were available to support them in such a short turnaround time. In an elearning environment, this type of mandate was catastrophic because, realistically, it can take several months to build brand-new, engaging, and interactive courses. Without appropriate transition times for launching new curricula in online courses, media-rich courses are replaced with temporary just-in-time, "get it up quickly to meet the mandate" courses. Proper testing of the new learning environment cannot occur pre-launch, and in some cases, students will have lessons changing in courses while active in their program.

So as an organizational leader, what do you do when the authorities regulating your education and training program measure and enforce system policies derived from best practices for bricks-and-mortar schools?

It's important to remember that program inspectors are not your enemy (but are maybe a frenemy); instead, they are here to help ensure learners receive a quality education. That said, there are a few strategies you can use to work with them while still driving innovation in your online programs.

Create a Strategic Plan

There are many ways to inspire regulatory authorities to work with you so you can meet any new program or accreditation requirements in an extended time frame that is more appropriate for elearning. One of the most successful methods I have used is to develop a strategic plan with corresponding launch dates to complete the mandated curriculum updates and building of new courses. Our organization then submitted this plan to the education and training officials responsible for oversight at our school. We provided extensive details on the amount of work to be performed so that our inspector could see all the activities which needed to take place to meet the new requirements.

This approach has been particularly popular with officials who may not extensively use technology in their daily life and work. They genuinely may not understand how much work goes into updating the curriculum in an online course. Providing them with a strategic plan and report demonstrates that your organization has expertise in what needs to be done. They can also use your report or plan to substantiate making reasonable extensions to your curriculum launch deadlines.

Meeting Standards Before Site Visits

The best way to deal with program inspectors is to ensure you meet all the necessary standards before they arrive on site. Otherwise, any efforts made in other areas may be overlooked because attention will be focused on bringing your program up to par. Make sure you have an up-to-date list of all applicable regulations and requirements to proactively adhere to before any potential visit to your online program or physical school. Doing so builds trust and confidence with inspectors, who can see for themselves that you are offering a quality education and training program that checks all the right boxes.

Build and Maintain a Relationship with Your Inspectors

Anyone who has ever managed an organization subject to a regulatory authority knows the value and importance of maintaining good relationships with inspectors and officials. In 2002, I took a one-year leave from teaching to see if I could build a small private school specializing in distance learning for high school students. My dream was to build a program where students could access specialty courses not offered in their local high school. Elearning was so new at this point that it did not exist in our area.

To be considered a legal school offering Ontario credits entirely online, I had to meet a comprehensive book of policy requirements which, of course, were designed for bricks-and-mortar schools. When I began reading the necessary policy manuals, it was clear that my ideas for pioneering a high school virtual learning program would require some next-level thinking outside the box. Luckily, our very first school inspector was a visionary, and she worked so hard with us to help us figure out how we could fit into regulations that weren't designed for online learning (thank you, Nadine). To date, she remains one of the best inspectors I have worked with. Were it not for her, I might have found myself on a drastically different career path.

Communicate Openly and Honestly

In order to get the best results when it comes to education program inspections, open and honest communication with inspectors is essential. Nobody has all the answers, and inspectors can often provide insight and suggestions to help take your educational programs to the next level. Be open and honest about your process for delivering quality education online, including any innovative strategies or approaches you're taking. This will help show your organization's commitment to providing quality education and staying within regulatory guidelines. Nobody knows your program better than you do, but an inspector can provide potential solutions and valuable advice in gaining and maintaining your accreditation status. It's always in your best interest to embrace an open channel of communication.

Sometimes You Need to Check the Box

During the process of establishing my first online school, there were times when we were asked to create policies and processes that had no relevance to our learning program simply so that the government could check a box on our school application form. For example, we were advised that to be an inspected private school in Ontario and be granted the ability to offer recognized credits to our learners; we needed to have a policy on administering medication to students. I explained that we did not and could not administer medication to students because we didn't have a physical school; students worked on their courses online. The response I received was a reiteration that a policy was required for us to become a legal school. So, although it was absurd, we created a policy, and the government checked its box.

As a pioneer in education technology, this was a theme we repeatedly encountered with regulatory authorities. We quickly learned that if we wanted to avoid being perpetually submerged in red tape and disputes, it was sometimes just easier to comply in a way that regulatory authorities would accept. This allowed us to move on to more important things (like developing exceptional learning).

Find a Champion–Join a Federation

An education federation is an organization that brings together schools and educators to share strengths and resources. When you join a Federation with other education and training organizations, you can get support from your colleagues and peers when new regulatory mandates are launched. In Ontario, Canada, many private schools will join an organization, such as the Ontario Federation of Independent Schools (OFIS). The Federation sets the standards for membership and will connect your organization with its network, where you can access shared resources and professional development and receive administrative and policy development support.

Membership in this type of alliance provides a range of benefits, such as cooperation between colleagues from nearby educational institutions, support for professional learning opportunities, access to improved technology and resources, and advocacy for common issues across the region. By joining a federation, educators can pool their resources, improve their skill sets and gain access to learning information and materials that would otherwise not be available to them. In addition, it also creates a larger network of professionals who can collaborate on larger-scale projects which require a collective effort. Ultimately, an education federation provides its members with increased influence over regional issues related to education.

If difficulties with regulatory authorities are encountered, the federation will become a champion for its members. If your organization challenges an unfair regulatory practice or policy on your own, you are a single voice that may often have little impact on officials' decision-making. A federation representing hundreds of education and training institutions and challenging an unfair government policy or practice is more likely to be heard since they represent a collaborative group of voices. The federation is also more likely to have established contacts and relationships with regulatory authorities and the media, allowing them to make better progress in disputing an issue. This kind of support can be lifesaving and ensures you are not unfairly navigating new regulatory policies alone.

A further benefit to being a member of a federation is that it will stay abreast of any new regulatory or curriculum changes being proposed that may affect you. This will help you stay tuned into your operating environment and avoid getting caught unaware by significant regulatory changes.

The Last Resort–Taking a More Assertive Approach

If all the above strategies have yet to work and you find your distance education organization in an impossible and unfair situation with a regulatory authority, sometimes it may become necessary to take a more assertive approach and seek a higher authority. The problem with this course of action is that you will likely burn a bridge, and you never really know how that might affect the future reality of your organization. Sometimes, however, you absolutely have no choice.

In one such incident, I had a phone call with our education official providing oversight for our school in response to receiving a letter from the Ministry of Education advising all schools that they had only 30 days to implement recent curriculum changes. In our instance, this would affect seven online courses and require massive redevelopment. We were still a small school, so we had only one instructional designer on our team to work with all of our instructors. I inquired with our inspector if any accommodations were being made for online schools to give us time to build the new courses required. He flatly said no (he was clearly not a fan of elearning). He expected us to meet any new curriculum mandate issued in the same timeline face-to-face classrooms would have to meet it.

The only possible way to do this would be to change lessons in live courses with students actively learning in them. Can you imagine participating in a course where there are new evaluation requirements and new lessons every day you log in? Such a strategy (or anti-strategy) for launching a new online curriculum falls into the crazyville category. It violates every principle of best practices for managing learning (online or otherwise) and, quite seriously, the principles of common sense. When I raised these issues to our education official, he responded, "How you get it done is not my problem." Good times.

So that left us with no alternative but to write one of those scary letters we've all had to write at one time or another to the Ministry of Education Director. It went something like this... "Your education official has instructed us to change the curriculum in live courses containing active students. This official has no background or qualifications in elearning, so if you would like me to do this, I would ask you to please send me a letter confirming that these are your directions in writing."

Let's face it, officials can sometimes use their power poorly on the phone, but they never want to put it in writing. We ended up with a new education inspector, to our great relief. However, as an interesting sidebar, I saw our former official a couple of years later when I was providing a training session to the Ministry of Education school inspectors on best practices for elearning. He was one of my audience of learners—I file this one under funny but super-awkward moments.

Conclusion

Working with program inspectors isn't easy, but it doesn't have to be impossible either. By following some simple strategies like creating a strategic plan, meeting relevant standards ahead of time, building good relationships, communicating openly and honestly, and joining a federation for your type of program, organizational leaders can navigate program inspections while still innovating their virtual distance education and training offerings.

Leadership Questions

1. What types of program inspectors and accrediting bodies provide oversight for your virtual education and training program?

2. How can your team leaders proactively work with inspectors to ensure compliance and innovation?

3. Are there independent federations or organizations you can join to help represent and champion your efforts with regulatory authorities as part of a collaborative group?

Academic Fraud

Academic fraud or misconduct can be a costly threat to your organization, affecting the efficient delivery of your education and training program and the public's trust in the program and certifications you provide. Lack of integrity and unethical behavior in distance education is inconsistent with its primary purpose: To provide increased and equivalent access to learning opportunities for all.

Academic fraud is now a business that generates millions of dollars globally each year. It's important for organizational leaders to stay vigilant and take steps to ensure that their online learning programs are secure and free of academic fraud. Failing to target and control academic misconduct in your virtual education and training program can be a career-ending, business-destroying act that can ruin your organization's reputation. Universities and colleges have their own systems for evaluating students coming from private programs. Frequent or major cases of academic misconduct can cause the devaluing or delisting of your program with partners, clients, learners, and accreditation authorities.

Academic fraud has been increasing in both face-to-face and online distance education classrooms. Access to the Internet and electronic devices has made monitoring academic fraud a task of increasing difficulty for instructors and organizations. Websites like paperhelp.org, writemyessay.me, and papersowl.com make opportunities for learner plagiarism readily available. These sites and many more will write custom essays for students for a fee. There are also services where those writing standardized exams can obtain both the questions and the answers.

What Are the Most Common Types of Academic Fraud?

Academic fraud or misconduct is any form of cheating that occurs within an educational environment, whether physical or digital. It can range from using unauthorized materials (like cheat sheets) during a test or exam to getting someone else to complete an assignment. In virtual learning environments, academic fraud can take many forms, such as plagiarism, misrepresentation of work, or the use of false identities.

Different classifications of academic fraud can result from both intended, premeditated and unintended academic misconduct. For example:

- **plagiarism** – claiming someone else's work or ideas as your own;

- **cheating** – looking at someone else's work during an exam or test;

- **self-plagiarism** – submitting the same piece of work for credit in more than one course without the instructor's permission;

- **impersonating another person** – having another person write a test or exam in your place (or being the person who writes a test in someone else's place), either in person or online;

- **purchasing essays and assignments** – having a person or business write an assignment or complete a project for you;

- **falsifying or misrepresenting an academic record or supporting documents** – forging documents to gain admission to an educational program is considered academic misconduct and will cause either revocation of an offer of admission or expulsion from an academic program if discovered at a later date;

- **use of unauthorized aids during a test or exam** – this includes anything not cleared or approved by an instructor for use during an exam.

- **improper access to materials** – this can be getting an advance copy of a term paper or test through theft or selling/distributing a term paper or test.

Motivation for Academic Misconduct

An individual's motivation to commit academic fraud may vary according to their demographic and sometimes geographic profile. Younger learners rarely conduct a cost-benefit analysis before cheating on a test or submitting a plagiarized paper. They may have left things to the last minute, fearing failure or feeling pressure at home to succeed. I have often found this to be true with students attending schools internationally, especially if their parents pay tuition fees for them to participate in an educational program.

Adult professionals may find themselves in high-stakes situations where credentialing requirements change or become increasingly competitive and yet are required for occupational, income, and social advancement.

In some instances, there are also bricks-and-mortar organizations providing educational support services that will, unfortunately, create an environment of academic misconduct. I have had cases with education centers providing tutoring services whereby parents paid tutors significant fees to provide educational support for online high school courses. The tutors would save copies of our randomized tests for future students to study from. They also ensured that all papers completed by students were only submitted once they were A-grade papers. Thus, papers were not created independently by students. Sometimes there was a significant gray area in these practices where the tutor was not actually writing the essay for the student. Still, students were "over-tutored" and could not succeed on course evaluations independently.

The Academic Fraud Autopsy

Over time, we develop virtual education street smarts. Almost every instructor on the planet has had a learner pull the wool over their eyes at some point (myself included). If I look back to the beginning of my elearning career, when the ideologies and technologies for online instruction were in their infant phases, I was comparable to Bambi wandering into the woods. I had yet to learn of the illegitimate lengths some learners would go to in order to pass a course successfully.

All it takes is one publicized incident of massive academic fraud to erode the confidence of the academic community, learners, and parents. This means the qualifications and competence of learners leaving your program may be questioned. Thus, if you discover an incident where a learner or group of learners has successfully gotten away with major academic fraud in your education and training program, you will need your team to take it seriously. A complete autopsy of what occurred needs to be conducted so that you can strengthen your policies and practices to help prevent any future incidences.

It Can Erode Your Credibility
In our early years operating as a distance education school, we had one such incident we had to deal with. My school guidance official advised me that a university had called because five international students enrolled in our program had obtained similar marks in the 90th percentile in their grade 12 university preparation English course. When reviewing the students' files and transcript history, it was noted that English was a second language, and they had barely passed previous high school English courses. The grade 12 university

preparation English course was challenging. Although it was always possible the learners achieved such high marks because, when working at their own pace, there was more time to master course concepts, it was doubtful and unprecedented. Upon receiving the news, I think my stomach hit the floor, and I cracked open a bottle of antacids.

As a new distance education school specializing in high school credits and pioneering with technology, we had to work double time to demonstrate the credibility of our program. Although distance education courses and credits are widely accepted today, fifteen years ago, the academic community deemed diplomas achieved through elearning highly suspect.

An incidence of academic fraud with five students entering the same university program could cripple our credibility as a distance-learning provider. As we began our academic autopsy to investigate the incident (and determine if the credits were obtained legitimately), it became pretty clear they were not. So our first question was why the instructor had not picked up on any of the anomalies we had found, especially since we provided a license for *Turnitin,* a plagiarism detection system, for all our instructors and classes. The same instructor was responsible for all five students. We determined that several factors played into what had transpired:

- **Failure to Use Available Tools** – although we provided our instructors with a license for Turnitin, this particular teacher simply wasn't using it. She either didn't have the time or motivation to submit her students' papers through the system.

- **Discomfort with Learning New Technologies** – had the instructor engaged in this single activity, she would have known her students were cheating. As it turned out, she wasn't entirely comfortable using the plagiarism software but had been too shy to let us know she needed additional help or training.

The Role of Academic History

The instructor in the previous example also did not have access to the students' academic history to know that their current achievement levels were vastly higher than their overall academic averages. Whether instructors should have access to a student's educational history is a controversial topic. Many factions believe that a student's current academic studies should not be mitigated or judged by their past performance academically. There is a fear that if an instructor views a student as a low performer historically, it will influence the perception of what the student can achieve in future courses. And although I agree with this principle, in my viewpoint, if a student is achieving marks that are 40% higher than any that have been achieved before in the same subject area, an alarm needs to go off for the instructor.

Creating a Culture of Academic Integrity

The first step any online learning program should take is to create an academic integrity policy that clearly outlines what constitutes acceptable behavior and the consequences for violating the policy. You'll want to make sure you prominently display the policy on your website so that all students are aware of it upon registering for courses. You will also want to ensure your instructors are familiar with and understand how to enforce the policy properly.

There can be many ambiguities and perceptions between regions and cultures about what actually constitutes academic fraud. In countries like Malaysia, where the educational system is based solely on standardized testing, it is common practice for instructors to teach to the test and to do whatever is necessary to prepare students to write the standardized tests.

Therefore, it may not be viewed as academic misconduct to prepare one student to write a test using questions from a previous student's test a few days before or to find and illegitimately purchase test banks from publishers which are to be sold only to educators with the supporting textbook for a course. I have had to address this issue with some international schools, and they were genuinely shocked and surprised that their actions were considered academic misconduct in the North American education system.

For this reason, your organization must have clear policies and guidelines on what constitutes academic dishonesty and what consequences or penalties you will enforce should it occur.

Ten Strategies for Combating Academic Dishonesty

There are many strategies organizations can employ to combat academic dishonesty. The following are a few we found to be particularly successful in our virtual learning programs.

1. The Academic Oath of Honor

In 2014, Harvard College in the US voted to establish their institution's first-ever honor code. An honor code requires that students pledge they are aware of their schools' academic dishonesty policies and solemnly swear to conduct themselves to uphold their school's honor code.

In our elearning program, students had to sign an academic oath of honor before commencing any courses with us. They also had to sign a similar academic pledge of honor at the end of their course, just before they would write their final exam. I think signing an academic oath immediately before their final exam positively affected learners who were already nervous if they attended planning to cheat. It may have made them rethink things while reminding them of the severe and rigid consequences of any act of academic dishonesty. We also required any staff member at a local or foreign learning center working with our students to sign an academic oath of honor before commencing any partnership with our distance education program. This ensured they knew precisely what constituted academic misconduct in our North American education system.

I was initially skeptical whether an oath of honor would really change or impact learner attempts at academic dishonesty at our school; however, the results were quite astounding. Overall academic fraud attempts dropped by 50% in the first year after instituting our honor code. Having students, parents, and partners sign our honor code fostered a stronger sense of responsibility, trust, and academic integrity in our learning community.

2. Promote Open Communication Between Students & Instructors

One of the most effective ways to prevent academic dishonesty is by encouraging open communication between instructors and learners throughout each course session. Students should feel comfortable asking questions about any assignment instructions that may be unclear or confusing. This will help them avoid inadvertently committing academic fraud by misunderstanding the guidelines. On a related note, instructors should also be aware of signs of academic dishonesty, such as sudden changes in grades or performance levels, as this could indicate that a student has been receiving outside assistance with their work.

3. Plagiarism Detection Systems

Many plagiarism detection systems are now available to organizations delivering education and training programs. Some are smaller systems that are inexpensive and intended for individual teachers with smaller classes. Others are larger systems that can be used in organizations with thousands of learners.

One of my favorite systems to work with to date has been *turnitin.com*. One thing I like about Turnitin is that it has a variety of license options. As noted earlier in this chapter, a plagiarism detection system can only work if instructors use it in their courses. You also can have students upload their assignments into the system, after which it issues a plagiarism report to both the student and instructor. This accomplishes two things:

- **Reduces Instructor Workload** – if an instructor has 50 students and very little free time, they do not have to be constantly uploading individual assignments into the system;

- **Increases Student Responsibility** – since the student also receives a copy of the report, they learn what constitutes plagiarism, allowing them to evolve and grow as learners.

Plagiarism detection systems like turnitin.com work by maintaining a comparison database that consists of the following:

- current and archived Internet content;
- books, newspapers, journals, library databases, digital reference collections, and subscription-based publications;
- all other student papers submitted to Turnitin from other institutions around the world.

After receiving a submission, Turnitin creates an originality report showing the degree of similarity between a submitted assignment and the sources of the written content used in a paper.

4. Learning Analytics

As mentioned earlier in this book, learning analytics from your LMS provides data on how often your learners access their course, their navigation, and learning patterns. You can use various tools available in your LMS to determine if a learner has legitimately completed a course or program you are offering. For example, detailed course statistics are available in Moodle. These can inform you if a student writes a test but hasn't viewed the lessons in their course which correspond to the test (definite academic fraud flag). You can see how frequently a student logs into their course, the pages they navigate, and even the IP address from which they are accessing their program. We had a case of multiple students attempting to cheat on the same test. By viewing their IP addresses, we noted they all wrote the test from the same location—a local learning center perpetuating academic misconduct. We thus flagged the center and accepted no future student enrollments from them.

5. Randomized Tests, Quizzes, and Exams

Most learning management systems will allow you to create randomized tests where the questions selected for each learner are drawn from a bank of hundreds or thousands of questions. For this strategy to work effectively, you must be able to establish large test banks for your courses. If you use instructor resources from a publisher for courses such as math or science, you can typically purchase the test banks corresponding to your course textbook. Test banks, however, are not infallible. Instructors must review test bank questions before they are loaded for a course to ensure they are good questions *relevant* to the learning material provided. The textbook is a supporting resource for the course, and few courses involve having learners cover every single page of a textbook (or at least they shouldn't). Therefore, it makes sense that only some questions available in a test bank will apply to a course you are offering. Sometimes, questions developed by a third party who is not the instructor for a course may not make sense to learners or be relevant to their country or culture.

If you are offering a course for which no test bank is available, then one strategy we used was to have our instructors create a predesignated number of questions each month to begin developing a question pool. This ensured it would grow over time and prevent questions from being compromised as multiple students in various geographic locations accessed the test. Another flag then came up. Students attempting academic fraud would sometimes score very high on questions being utilized from the bank for more than a year and then score poorly only on newly created questions from the instructor. In this type of occurrence, it was evident that someone had shared questions from previous tests or somehow purchased the test bank (which is only supposed to be sold to academic institutions). Accordingly, we would check to see if the student was working with a learning center and then flag the center to monitor other students who were also attending it.

Another great feature of randomized tests is that if learners are taking the test in a lab with side-by-side computers, they all receive different questions in a different order and cannot copy from someone sitting close by.

6. Evaluations Requiring a Learner to Produce a Unique Piece of Work

If a test is composed of questions with static answers which do not vary (for example, 2+2 = 4), then all students will submit the same answer to this question. This can make it very difficult to detect when academic fraud is occurring. But if a student is asked to write a short story or blog post, each student will submit a unique result for their assignment. Understandably, not all courses are conducive to having students produce unique works as evidence of content mastery. However, it is incredible what instructors can come up with. For example, I had one instructor ask students to conduct a science experiment at home using kitchen chemistry (safe ingredients) and to video the results. This type of assessment is very difficult, if not impossible, to plagiarize.

7. Providing Oral Evaluations

One of the most common questions I used to receive in our elearning program was, "How do we know for sure the student who completed a test or evaluation was the same student enrolled in the course?" One strategy instructors would use to validate a student's coursework was creating an oral evaluation during the course, conducted through videoconferencing. An oral evaluation makes it clear whether a learner is submitting their own work. By conducting this type of evaluation, an instructor could obtain a general idea of how much knowledge a learner had attained in the course material. They could then assess whether the results of the oral evaluation corresponded with the online evaluations the learner achieved throughout the course.

8. Supervised Exams

Digital exam proctoring allows for location-independent testing while maintaining exam results' integrity. There are two types of virtual proctoring:

- **Remote proctoring** – this is real-time proctoring where a person actively supervises a learner online throughout their test. It is typically used for major evaluations such as final examinations for a course, as the costs to have every learner assessment proctored live would be extremely high. The reliability and integrity of the results are heavily dependent on the remote supervisor and the number of learners they supervise at any one time. It can be very tedious for an instructor to supervise 20 learners for two hours on a Zoom Screen. However, this is also true of exams supervised in person.

- **Automated proctoring** – this is wholly automated proctoring conducted using machine learning and facial detection technology. With automated proctoring, the reliability and integrity of results depend on the technology used. There have been many cases of flawed proctoring results after students received a grade of zero on their online exam after reading the questions aloud or got locked out of their test because they had a poor Internet connection. There have also been issues with faulty facial recognition software being unable to recognize people of color. Remote proctoring can be a game changer as it is limitlessly scalable, but only if technology systems can overcome these issues.

It should also be noted that the transition to digital proctoring, be it live or automated, can be very stressful for students. Many become worried about having no recourse when an automated system performs proctoring. The potential for systems to unjustly flag events when no violations have occurred can be a valid concern. Relying solely on technology without human oversight significantly increases learner stress and may perpetuate distrust in exam results.

Some remote proctoring systems collect detailed personal information, including student images, sounds, and movements, throughout the testing process. This raises privacy concerns and can leave already anxious students intensely aware that their every move is being judged, whether by a machine or an instructor watching and listening from a remote location.

9. Adding a Timer to Open Book Tests

One strategy we used early on (before the existence of digital proctoring systems) to conduct evaluations was to create a timer for tests. This strategy, although imperfect, is still valid today. When creating a timed test, the instructor assumes a learner is at home working on an assessment without supervision. They will have access to all their books and materials, but not for an infinite period of time.

The downside is that a student could obtain assistance from a parent or friend. Thus, this type of evaluation should be used in conjunction with the overall assignments and exams for a course to get a reliable idea of learner mastery of course content and their overall achievement levels. When there is a significant discrepancy between proctored and non-proctored evaluations, organizations tend to rely more heavily on evidence of achievement from the proctored evaluations or oral exams.

Another disadvantage can occur if the timer used for a course test does not have a discreet design. I visited one organization using a timer for their tests, and after logging in to review their system, I noted that the timer looked like a big square flag on the bottom right-hand side of the screen. Not only did it display a countdown of the minutes left in the test, it actually displayed the seconds—wowsers! I can tell you that if their learners were not anxious before starting their test, they would definitely have a panic attack trying to concentrate with a D-day end-of-time countdown happening at the bottom of their screen. Timers should be easy to access, blend into the background, and be discreet. The best ones I've seen have a show/hide option, count down in five-minute increments, and only move to a one-minute increment countdown in the last five minutes of the test.

10. Providing Varied Opportunities for Assessment and Evaluation

The best way to ensure the integrity of your program and any credits or certifications you issue is to offer your learners many evaluation opportunities as they progress through your program. This also ensures that your program provides varied evaluation opportunities to learners who perform better in some types of evaluations than others. For example, some learners might do better on a multiple-choice quiz, while others are better at writing their thoughts on essay-style questions. Varied assessment opportunities ensure assessments:

- are fair, transparent, and equitable for all learners and are communicated clearly to students at the beginning of each course;

- are different in nature and administered over a period of time to provide multiple opportunities for learners to demonstrate the full range of their course mastery;

- support all students, including those with special education needs.

If a student achieves consistent results after taking an online quiz, submitting a unique assignment, completing an oral test with their instructor, and taking a proctored final exam, you can be reasonably sure their results are reliable.

Academic Misconduct Disciplinary Measures

Once you have created your code of conduct for academic integrity at your organization, you will also need to determine what consequences you will assign in cases of academic dishonesty or academic misconduct.

Many factors should be taken into account when considering what sanctions should be imposed on the learner who is guilty of academic dishonesty. For example, younger learners require an opportunity to learn and grow from their mistakes so they can move forward to continue their studies. However, in an adult learner, where brains are fully developed, and we should decidedly know better, the consequences of academic fraud are typically more severe. Most institutions will consider a range of disciplinary measures with varying levels of severity, including:

- **resubmission** – having a student redo an assignment;

- **grade of zero** – receiving a failing grade on an assignment or test; or

- **dismissal** – having more severe consequences, such as suspension or expulsion from your program.

Different Perceptions of Academic Misconduct

Education is a fundamental and global good that helps us all grow as we travel our journey in life. When I began my elearning journey as an educator, I believed we should enforce disciplinary measures in cases of academic misconduct; however, they should not be so severe as to prevent students from learning from their mistakes and being given another chance to continue their studies. I genuinely believe access to quality ongoing education and training opportunities can change the world. When people make mistakes, the worst thing we can do as educators is to impose a sanction that completely removes learners from their learning journey. In international programs, many of our students came from developing countries where there were few opportunities to access quality education programs. Thus, when considering appropriate disciplinary measures in a case of academic misconduct, the expulsion of a young learner living in an area where they can not necessarily opt to attend another school (because there are no other schools) has to be taken with the utmost seriousness.

Organizational Policies Must Evolve

As the years progressed in my elearning career journey as the director of a distance learning school, so did my position on academic misconduct. I noticed some disturbing patterns with younger learners who committed academic fraud.

Our school policy initially held that we would give a student a zero on any assignment or test involving academic misconduct. Unfortunately, in almost 100% of cases where the only consequence was the student receiving a zero grade on the assignment, the student plagiarized again. This was unbelievable to me! Why didn't getting caught and facing shame and consequences at school and home while receiving a zero on an assignment deter future incidents?

Some teachers had the same students attempting to plagiarize repeatedly in their courses. They would receive a zero on one online assignment (have their parents notified, etc.) and then unfathomably try to plagiarize again on the very next assignment. This resulted in a great deal of stress, administration for our school, and a lot of extra work for instructors.

Upon investigation, we noted that some students doing this were coming from international learning partner centers. This made me suspect the centers were somehow taking part in perpetuating student academic dishonesty.

After much discussion and debate, our school added two additional consequences to our academic fraud policies:

1. Students who were guilty of an incidence of plagiarism or other forms of academic misconduct received a mark of zero on the assignment. They were also billed an administration fee of $150, which had to be paid before they could continue in any other courses in our program.

2. If a student was found guilty of a second incidence of academic fraud, they were expelled from their course. Since our students were of high school age, they could still enroll in other courses, which ensured they could continue accessing an education program (especially since they were living in a developing country with few educational opportunities available). But it was a significant consequence to the student, as it expelled them from a course they had paid full tuition fees to attend, and they would not receive a final course mark or credit. They had to pay the entire course tuition fees again to enroll in another course.

We instituted the new disciplinary measures, and our academic fraud instances were reduced by an unbelievable 80% over the next school year. And quite honestly, we weren't sure why. Yes, the new consequences of academic misconduct were more severe; however, in the grand scheme of things, the administration fee wasn't that much. International students spend thousands of dollars annually on tuition fees to access an accredited Canadian online pre-university program. Why did the $150 administration fee have such a significant impact on deterring academic fraud?

In essence, we determined that parents of international students rarely spoke English and thus relied solely on the international education center to support their children throughout the elearning program. Parents were happy as long as students received good marks and progressed through the program. Frequently, when an academic misconduct instance would occur, the local center did not notify parents, so they were oblivious to what was happening. Our establishment of the academic fraud administration fee required the center to notify parents, as this fee had to be paid before the student could continue the program. In these occurrences, parents were extremely angry with the centers, as they were supposed to provide program oversight and guidance to students.

As a Canadian distance education program, we could not possibly have anticipated these events. Still, we certainly learned from them, and they helped our academic misconduct policies and procedures evolve in a successful way, drastically reducing our instances of academic fraud. I sometimes think even here in Canada and the US; younger learners may engage in academic dishonesty in a distance education program and then somehow find a way to ensure their parents or guardians do not receive the notice from the school. Thus, elearning programs designed for students under the age of 18 must ensure parents and guardians are involved in their child's progress.

Conclusion

Academic fraud is a serious problem in both physical and virtual educational environments, and it's essential organizational leaders take measures to prevent it in their online learning programs. Preventing academic fraud and misconduct is no small task. It requires diligence from both educators and organizational leaders alike. Establishing an effective honor code and incorporating technology-based solutions like plagiarism detectors and digital proctoring services can go a long way toward effectively combating this issue in your distance education and training program.

Leadership Questions

1. What steps can you take to ensure that your online learning programs are secure and free of academic fraud?

2. What are the potential consequences of an academic misconduct case for your organization's reputation?

3. What do you feel should be the key components of your academic integrity policy for your distance education and training program?

4. What will be the consequences of violating your academic integrity policies?

5. What strategies and technologies will your organization employ to combat academic dishonesty?

ELEARNING GOLD—ANNETTE LEVESQUE

Security Screening When Hiring Your Distance Learning Team

A few decades ago, it was common practice for employers to hire people based on resumes and references. However, the hiring process has become much more complex in today's world. If you're considering hiring remote and virtual employees, you must ensure your security measures are up to par.

An unfortunately common potential security vulnerability you will want to consider when hiring teachers and instructors is identity theft. It is now essential for organizations to conduct a thorough security screening of each potential employee before hiring them. This is especially important for roles that involve working with vulnerable groups like children or the elderly. But why is this process so important?

One crucial issue is related to regulatory authorities for various professions, including teachers now posting teacher information and credentials online. For example, in Ontario, this is conducted by the Ontario College of Teachers (OCT). The intent behind this is to create transparency so parents and administrators can look up any teacher in Ontario online to view their education history, diplomas, and academic achievements. They may also view any complaints which may have been launched.

In today's world, however, this makes it very easy for someone to adopt a teacher's identity since OCT publicly provides all their credential information online. This means someone can illegitimately apply for a teaching position with a resume that will detail accurate education information for the teacher they are trying to impersonate.

I worked with one school where learners were required to write a supervised exam in their home country via an exam proctor with specific credentials. A learner submitted a false resume, with real teaching credentials, for the instructor who was to be supervising their exam in an attempt to commit academic fraud. They even went so far as to create a fake email address for the exam proctor using their real name.

Administrators or human resources staff hiring employees and instructors working remotely from home in your organization's distance education program must be highly cautious when reviewing resumes and credentials. You must develop solid hiring policies and procedures which are strictly adhered to, without exception. You can take several steps to protect your organization and learners, including:

- **ID Verification** – ensure an instructor or employee's identification matches the information on their SIN card (Canada) or their Social Security card (U.S.);

- **Background Check** – require that prospective employees provide a recent criminal background check;

- **References** – require that at least two references be organization-based and have an HR staff member call each reference (instead of just emailing them);

- **Video Interviews** – conduct your interview using video conferencing software so that you can see that the person applying to work for your organization matches the photo on the submitted identifications.

It is of utmost importance for your organization to take a proactive approach to validate the credentials of distance education staff working in your education and training program. Creating policies and procedures for screening prospective staff and raising awareness amongst those who do your hiring will create an environment with proper oversight and controls. This helps protect your organization and learners from potential ill-meaning persons attempting to assume an identity or commit fraud for short-term gain.

Conclusion

It's important for your organization to prioritize safety above all else when hiring new virtual instructors and staff for your distance education and training program. Running background checks, verifying educational credentials and employment history, and checking references are all great ways to ensure that your organization only hires trustworthy individuals committed to providing quality services. This ensures a safe virtual learning environment for instructors and students.

Leadership Questions

1. Does your organization have policies and procedures for screening new potential hires working remotely from home?

2. Are there any additional measures you should implement to enhance your security protocols during your hiring process?

Creating a Distance Learning Strategic Plan

ELEARNING GOLD—ANNETTE LEVESQUE

Why Do We Need a Strategic Plan?

Launching a virtual learning portal can be an intimidating task. There are a lot of moving pieces, and it's easy to feel overwhelmed by the process. The key is to remember that you don't have to do it alone; in fact, you shouldn't. Creating a strategic plan is one of the best ways to ensure success. But why should you bother? Let's look at some benefits of having a strategic plan for your virtual learning portal launch.

Strategic planning is when leaders create a documented map of their vision for their organization's goals and how they will reach them. A strategic plan typically helps to define and share the direction an organization will take in the next three to five years.

A Strategic Plan Keeps You on Track

One of the biggest benefits of having a strategic plan is that it keeps you on track. It helps you stay focused on your goals and objectives while ensuring that all stakeholders are working toward a common goal. A good strategic plan should include timelines, specific tasks and deliverables, and milestones that will help keep everyone accountable and on time.

A Strategic Plan Helps You Identify Resources

When launching any project, it's essential to have access to the right resources. That could mean anything from personnel to materials or technology—the list goes on. A good strategic plan should include assessing what resources are needed for the project to be successful. This will help ensure that nothing falls through the cracks and will give you an idea of what new resources may need to be acquired for your virtual learning portal launch to succeed.

A Strategic Plan Sets Expectations

Having realistic expectations is key when launching any project—especially one as complex as a virtual learning portal launch! A good strategic plan should include expectations for each stakeholder involved in the project, including deadlines and deliverables and any potential roadblocks or challenges they may face along the way. This will help set clear expectations from the beginning, which can go a long way toward keeping everyone on track and motivated throughout the launch process.

Balancing Planning & Action

In my youth, as a business owner, I used to cringe at the thought of creating a strategic plan. It seemed like a great deal of uncomfortable, time-consuming hard work which, after being presented to my team, would end up forgotten in a desk drawer somewhere, gathering dust. And let's face it, the one thing new business owners and leaders are in short supply of is time to prepare yet more documentation.

I was not alone in these feelings. Many organizations develop elearning visions and mental project plans that are never implemented, sometimes because they are so complicated and time-consuming that it just seems impossible to make them happen. This is why some teams resist planning—they want to move into action and get things done. Sometimes situations can also create a sense of urgency requiring that we immediately propel into action, influenced by external circumstances beyond our control.

In the current state of our nation, a global pandemic has forced many businesses, schools, and post-secondary institutions into the rapid launch of elearning and online projects without the appropriate timelines typically required for executing such a massive organizational change. For these reasons, skipping the planning phase when launching new distance education projects can be very tempting. This can be detrimental to the overall project success and the financial and human resources burden placed on an organization.

However, when it comes to new distance education projects, developing a solid strategic plan is unbelievably important, as it helps us map out our project vision on paper before taking the ultimate personal and professional risk of launching it. It is said that if you fail to plan, you plan to fail. In these times, organizations must find the sweet spot that combines the elements of both planning and action (Woosley, 2013).

Begin With the End in Mind

Stephen Covey tells us we should always begin with the end in mind, so what is it you would like to teach and provide to your learners? What kind of learning experience would you like participants in your education and training program to have? What goal(s) should they expect to achieve upon successfully completing your degree or certification program? In other words, what should they be able to do, and what new knowledge and skill sets should they have attained?

    The strategic plan for your organization should outline the goals and objectives essential for your elearning project's success while creating a guideline of tasks and resources required to accomplish those goals and objectives. Implementation of this plan needs to focus on the prerequisites and constraints to be observed for the effective establishment of your program while also exploring potential risks and threats to be addressed. The overall plan is designed to guide your organization in achieving its desired elearning vision.

Conclusion

Having a solid strategy in place before launching your virtual learning portal can make all the difference between success and failure. It helps keep everyone accountable and ensures everyone on your team is heading in the same direction toward achieving your virtual learning goals. Plus, it has other benefits, such as helping identify resources needed for success, setting expectations for stakeholders involved in the project, and keeping everyone focused on their objectives throughout the process.

Leadership Questions

1. Does your organization have an up-to-date strategic plan in place as a guideline for achieving your desired vision for your distance education and training program?

2. How do you currently communicate your vision and goals to your team members and organization stakeholders?

Getting Started – How to Create a Simple Strategic Plan (SSP)

In this section, we will review the steps in creating a Simple Strategic Plan for the building or relaunching of your organization's virtual education and training world.

Most strategic plans are created when launching or considering a new business; however, the same principles apply when approaching a new project of significance that will affect your organization in a major way. Adding elearning and training capabilities to any organization is a significant undertaking and definitely fits under this umbrella. Most of us envision creating a strategic plan as a vast, complicated, and arduous process, but it need not be.

On his website "Conquer Your Kryptonite" James Woosley provides templates that can be very useful in developing what he refers to as a Simple Strategic Plan (SSP). Completing your strategic plan will provide transparency and direction to your stakeholders and ensure your project is completed and delivered within your desired timelines. You'll communicate your elearning vision and project goals in a way that makes sense to your team members. More importantly, defining your project strategy and measuring your progress throughout your project ensures you are hitting your key goals. In this chapter, we will adapt the Woosley SSP's primary principles for your elearning project plan.

Step 1–The SWOT Analysis

If you're an organizational leader, chances are you've heard of SWOT analysis—but do you know what it is and why it's important? A SWOT (strengths, weaknesses, opportunities, and threats) analysis is a handy tool that can help you, as a leader, make informed decisions when launching your new virtual learning program. Do you know your organization's strengths and weaknesses as they relate to launching your new elearning project?

We all feel our hearts beat just a little faster, and our palms sweat when we hear the term "SWOT analysis." For the leader about to embark into what feels like the unknown Wild West of technology and elearning, the SWOT sounds like an exercise that will be about as much fun as preparing for tax season. It definitely requires some thought and reflection and a little homework, but I promise you will knock this part of your strategic plan out of the park in no time.

Why Use a SWOT Analysis?

Conducting a thorough SWOT analysis before launching any new distance learning project can help leaders identify potential risks and maximize their chances of success. It also allows them to think through all their options and consider how best to use their resources. By looking at internal and external factors, leaders can gain valuable insights into the current state of the market. This information can then be used to their advantage when making decisions about their future distance learning program offerings.

By taking the time to conduct this type of assessment before diving into any new venture, leaders can ensure they have considered every angle, thus increasing their chances of success. Let's break down the components of a SWOT analysis and discuss why it's essential to use this tool before launching or redesigning your distance education and training program.

Internal vs. External Factors

The strengths and weaknesses component of the SWOT analysis refers to those that are internal to your organization—they are items you likely have some control over and can change. Examples might include who is on your team, your patents and intellectual property, and your location.

Opportunities and threats refer to external factors and things going on outside your organization in the larger market. Examples include competitors, prices of raw materials, changes in your legal and regulatory environment, and customer buying trends—or perhaps a very unexpected and surreal and crazy global pandemic event. You can take advantage of opportunities and protect against threats, but you can't change them.

Building your SWOT chart is the first step in building your elearning vision. Your SWOT analysis will organize your top strengths, weaknesses, opportunities, and threats into an organized list, usually presented in a simple two-by-two grid (Parsons, 2019). Try to be as honest as possible in assessing each area—make it a brainstorming exercise for your team. The rest of your strategic plan will be built upon this exercise (Woosley, 2013).

Action Steps to Complete Your SWOT

You can use bullet points when completing each area of your SWOT chart.

1. **Strengths** – Make a list of your organization's internal strengths applicable to the launch of your elearning project. These would include any advantage, skill, proficiency, experience, talent, or other internal factors that improve your organization's position in executing your project. Examples might include:

    - solid financing or cash flow for your project;
    - a superior brand or level of accreditation;
    - valuable intellectual property;
    - superior technology, a well-trained instructional design team;
    - low staff turnover;
    - management expertise;

- operational efficiency;
- excellent partnerships and support, etc.

Write down what your organization and elearning team do inherently well (where are you remarkable?) and other factors working in your favor at this point in time. These are the good things that you can leverage to your advantage.

2. **Weaknesses** – These are the factors that reduce your organization's ability to achieve its objectives. Examples might include:

    - unreliable contractors;
    - outdated technology;
    - lack of funding;
    - management or leadership weaknesses;
    - gaps in expertise, etc.

Everybody will need to be as honest as they can when identifying these deficiencies. Ignoring organizational limitations means you can't make decisions that will strengthen the development and launch of your online learning project. List the things you don't or can't do well right now. These are areas you need to develop into minimum competencies, perhaps outsource to another expert or eliminate altogether as you move forward. They are present pains that can inhibit your progress.

3. **Opportunities** – Opportunities are potential influences, chances, and changes that may allow your project to grow and become successful. Examples might include new potential markets, innovations, technological advances, consumer trends, and support from governments, the community, or business partners. List the things that might take you to the next level once you have begun. What new resources can you tap into to get to the next level?

4. **Threats** – Threats are external obstacles that you must overcome. Threats may include a declining economy, technological change, a shortage of skill sets or the expertise you need to develop your project, community opposition, legal or regulatory changes, etc. List the things that are in your way or can take you down. You'll want to counter/eliminate these threats as you move forward with your plan.

Your SWOT analysis doesn't have to be a long, complex document. Two or three pages of point-form notes are usually sufficient (BDC, 2020).

Conclusion

Conducting a thorough SWOT analysis before building a new distance learning world is essential for organizational leaders looking to maximize their chances of success. This type of assessment helps identify potential risks while also giving leaders valuable insight into internal and external factors that could affect their project's outcome. Taking extra time beforehand to thoughtfully consider all aspects of your virtual learning project with your team will result in more informed decisions and ultimately lead to greater success when it's time to launch.

Leadership Questions

Once you've examined all four aspects of your completed SWOT analysis, you'll likely be faced with a list of potential actions. Taking it in as a whole, it's time to brainstorm the following questions with your team.

1. How can you build on your strengths?
2. What resources can you access to boost your weaker areas?
3. What measures can you take to head off any threats you have identified?
4. How can you take advantage of the opportunities you have discovered?

Step 2–Your Organization's Project Mission Statement

You are starting your new virtual world project and have a perfect idea, but you want to ensure everyone is on the same page. You need to craft a mission statement! But why should you create a mission statement when launching a new distance education and training project? Let's look at how this can help your team succeed.

A Clear Direction

A mission statement is your team's "North Star"—it provides clarity, direction, and focus for everyone involved in the project. It defines what your team will accomplish, who will be responsible for specific tasks, and what goals you should achieve by what date. A mission statement also helps ensure everyone has the same end goal in mind and makes it easier for them to work together as one cohesive unit.

Your mission statement for your elearning project taps into the passion behind the project and begins to define the dream. It outlines where you are now and your organization's underlying motivation for commencing with a new initiative. It spells out the contribution to the organization and society at large that the organization aspires to make in launching your elearning project. It defines your team's purpose and why your new virtual learning world should exist.

Setting Expectations

Having an agreed-upon mission statement helps set expectations from the very beginning of the project. Everyone knows what they need to do and how long they must do it to meet their deadlines. This eliminates confusion and encourages team members to stay on task while helping each other reach their goals. With clear expectations, everyone on the team knows exactly what they need to contribute to making progress toward completion.

Keeping Motivation High

Creating a mission statement also helps keep motivation high throughout the duration of the project. The mission statement serves as an ongoing reminder of why everyone is working together on this particular project, what impact it could have inside and outside your organization, and how you will measure success once it's complete. This can help ensure that every member of your team stays focused and motivated until completion.

What is Your Fundamental Purpose in Your Virtual World Project?

Ask yourself and your team the purpose and mission behind your project. For example, perhaps you would like to establish an electronic learning and training environment that is engaging and tailored to fit your exclusive education and learner needs. Or perhaps you aim to provide your employees with ongoing access to the best learning opportunities using modern technologies and resources. Your project mission statement should tell people what you do and why you do it. What is your fundamental purpose, and how will your new elearning project align with this purpose?

Tips for Creating an Effective Project Mission Statement

Your project mission statement is a declaration of what makes what you do and, by extension, your elearning project important. By design, it guides your team's actions and creates organizational direction by explaining what it intends to accomplish. Some tips to consider in your distance learning project mission statement:

- **Keep It Short and Concise.** Sum up your organizational project mission in just a few sentences.

- **Consult Your Team.** Find out what your team members think of the mission statement. Ask how they would improve it and what they dislike about it. Your mission statement should be designed with them in mind, so get their opinion.

- **Don't be Afraid to Change it**. Things change, and organizations must adapt and evolve in response to their operational needs and the external climate in which they operate. If the mission statement no longer represents the project intentions of your organization, it is time for a rewrite (BigCommerce, 2021).

Conclusion

Creating a mission statement should be at the top of your list when launching any new virtual learning project. It gives everyone involved with the project clarity, direction, focus, and motivation throughout its duration. Crafting a solid mission statement isn't always easy, but if done correctly, it can make all the difference in ensuring success.

Leadership Questions

1. What are the primary reasons your online education and training project should exist?

2. Does your mission statement easily communicate the purpose and mission behind your project?

Step 3—Your Core Values

Core values are specific extensions of your Mission Statement and define *why* you have set your organization's course in your desired direction for your distance education project. When examining your organization's core values, you will want to consider what your organization stands for, what you believe in and care about, and how, as an entity, you will behave.

Values are a lasting, passionate, and a distinctive set of core beliefs that are an essential part of developing your strategic plan. They are based on enduring tenets or guiding principles that your organization will adhere to no matter the obstacles you may encounter. Your core values are part of your strategic foundation. They are the beliefs that guide the conduct, activities, and goals of your organization and your team as you embark on your new elearning vision. They should establish why you do what you do and what you stand for.

Why Are Core Values Important?

The key to success in any project lies in understanding and adhering to your organization's core values. A team that understands the importance of its core values is better equipped to ensure that everyone involved in a project clearly understands their responsibilities and goals. Team members who understand their core values will also be more likely to remain motivated throughout a project because they are guided by principles they believe in and want to achieve.

Benefits of Strong Core Values

The expressed core values of your organization should reflect your deeply held convictions, priorities, and underlying assumptions that influence the attitudes and behaviors of your team members. Having strong core values accounts for why some organizations gain a reputation for such strategic traits as leadership and innovation. Your organization's values can dominate the strategic moves you decide to consider or reject. When your values and beliefs are deeply ingrained and widely shared by your directors, managers, and staff, they become a way of life within your organization. This will drive your organizational strategy as you move forward into a new frontier.

Role in Decision-Making

Your core values should also play an important role in decision-making during a project. As decisions are made, they should reflect the underlying principles of your organization's core values. This ensures that decisions are made with integrity and with the best interests of your organization in mind. It also effectively reminds team members that their actions should always reflect their commitment to achieving organizational goals.

Creating Meaningful Work

Organizational leaders must remember that launching a new project isn't just about meeting deadlines or fulfilling objectives; it's about creating meaningful work that aligns with your core values and reinforces them within your organization. Every successful project is an opportunity for your team members to demonstrate why they stand behind their organization's mission and how they can contribute toward achieving it.

Tips for Developing Your Core Values

1. You may want to categorize your Core Values as internal (what you value for yourself or within your business) or external (your values toward and on behalf of your customers).

2. Keep your list of values between five and seven, so they can be memorable to your team.

3. Create specific phrases for your core values; do not write paragraphs.

4. Your core values need to be shared. While you don't need a consensus from everyone in your organization, you do need some form of common agreement amongst your leadership and stakeholders (OnStrategy, 2019).

Some example core values related to your elearning project might be:

- Attract and recruit the finest distance education and technology experts in the world.

- Uphold the values and principles of best practices in distance education in every action and decision.

- Maintain the highest standards of elearning excellence with learners, team members, and your communities.

- Champion diversity as an essential component in the way you deliver your distance education and training program.

- Secure your future in the world of online education through innovation, creativity, and sustainability and by celebrating your successes as you proceed through the phases of launching your elearning vision.

Identifying Your Core Values

Many organizational leaders prefer to focus on hard numbers and the tasks and steps in their strategic plan rather than on the "soft" things such as values and culture. However, some of the largest organizations in the world have become so successful because of their understanding of the importance of core values as part of their organizational strategy.

If your organization and your people share the same values, you will:

- follow the same *rules*;
- establish the same *norms*;
- develop mutual *respect*;
- have similar *tolerances*;
- share *appreciation* (from a purpose and destination standpoint).

Values are an important component of the strategic planning process. If everyone has the same values, passion, and purpose, they will work together to realize your elearning goals (Taylor, 2016). Your core values will also allow you to explore the right opportunities to collaborate with other organizations, contractors, and vendors. To stay true to your values, those you work with and interact with will need to be in alignment with them (Woosley, 2013).

Conclusion

To have a successful distance education project, it is essential for your organization first to establish what your core values are. These values should be extensions of your organization's mission statement and help define why you've set your course in a desired direction. By focusing on these fundamental principles, you can ensure every decision made is guided by what matters most—your integrity and commitment to reaching your virtual learning goals.

Leadership Questions

1. What do you care about and believe in as a unified organization?

2. How does your elearning project align or connect with your core values?

3. Do your team members and other organizations you collaborate with align with your core values?

Step 4–Vision Statement

When launching a new virtual world project, every organizational leader wants to ensure it will succeed. But often, it's difficult to create that success without first having an end goal in mind. Creating a vision statement allows you to define the "why" behind your project—why are you doing this?

A vision statement is a clear and concise declaration of your organization's goals and mission, which will guide your team toward success. It gives clarity and direction and sets expectations for what we can realistically achieve. A well-written vision statement is something your organization should prepare before embarking on your new elearning journey. Let's look at why crafting one matters, its components, and how to effectively write your own.

Turning a Dream Into a Vision Statement

When I launched my first small school focused on providing accredited distance learning courses for high school students, it resulted from a vision. I had been working in the public school system as a teacher and had pioneered the launch of the board's first online courses. However, student access to these courses was riddled with red-tape-style obstacles. And even if a student could jump through the myriad of hurdles created by the public funding model to access an online course, the Ministry of Education itself was not ready to support this type of learning. I remember the day we excitedly

Creating a Distance Learning Strategic Plan

had four online courses ready to launch for the new school semester. Just a few days before the start date, we received a memo from the Ministry of Education stating they would not fund any day-school students enrolled in online courses. At that moment, despite our preparatory work, our elearning program was effectively squashed.

I began to dream about creating a way for students to access the online courses they needed outside the restrictions of the public funding model. Could I launch these courses privately, obtain accreditation, make them affordable for parents, and sustain my income level as a teacher? Launching a school that offered only elearning courses had never been done in our area, and it seemed both impossible and crazy at the time.

As my vision evolved, I made a formal plan and took a one-year leave of absence to build a small private school that would offer these courses to students. With the help of a very forward-thinking school inspector, I launched my first private high school, offering only four online courses, from my home office in 2002. Within the first year, I was by far exceeding my income as a public school teacher ($38k a year wasn't a huge milestone) and hired an office assistant and two other teachers to build courses with me. To my amazement, the program was a massive hit with students, parents, and other schools. Students who needed to take a high school course credit their local school was not offering could simultaneously enroll in it online while completing their other classroom courses. Each year, my vision grew, and

I had to learn to communicate it in a more formal way to my team, parents, and students.

What Is the Purpose of my Project? Why Should It Exist?

Your vision statement is based on future casting and outlines where you see your elearning project long-term down the road. It should be tangible and reflect the specific mountain you are currently trying to climb or the "where." Your organizational vision should define what is possible and provide a clear mental picture of where your project is heading in the long term. Your vision needs to be attractive, challenging, and compelling. It should reflect your organizational mission and the core values you outlined in the previous steps of your plan.

Your vision should be big enough to challenge you. In the land of entrepreneurs, we sometimes refer to visions as big-hairy-audacious-goals or BHAGs. They often seem to be very lofty at the time they are established. You and your team should stand in awe of your vision because it's real and probably scary—but achievable once documented!

Back to Your Why

Your vision statement takes you back to your why. In establishing your vision, you must first determine what type of elearning program you wish to establish. Is it an academic program designed for pre-university, university, or college students? Or is it a corporate learning/training program for either your employees or members of another organization? Will participants receive a diploma, degree, or certification after completing your program? What do you want the outcome to be when they have completed your program, and what do you expect them to learn?

Why do you want to begin your elearning project, and what is the ultimate impact that you want it to have on your organization and the greater world? What makes you think that embarking into the elearning world will be worth the investment of time, energy, and resources?

Academic Diploma Program or Corporate Learning?

Academic programs provide learners with the fundamental knowledge and skills they will need in their future adult lives and the opportunity to specialize in and explore areas related to their postsecondary goals and personal interests. Corporate learning focuses on a range of areas: learning to meet organizational goals, how to relate to fellow workers, and skills and competencies training for a specific employment role.

Tips for Creating Your Vision Statement

1. **Brainstorming** – the first step in crafting an outstanding vision statement is brainstorming ideas with your elearning team and colleagues. What do you want to accomplish? Are there values you wish to uphold? What's the focus of the project? Take all of these questions into consideration and start jotting down some ideas. This will create a foundation for the rest of the process.

2. **Refining & Editing** – now that you have some ideas, it's time to refine them and truly get down to the core of what matters most for this project. Ask yourself if each point is necessary and relevant to achieving your elearning goal. Is there anything that you could say better or more efficiently? Once you have streamlined everything, edit for grammar and readability. Make sure nothing is confusing or out of place so everyone involved understands exactly what the vision statement means.

3. **Making It Actionable** – forming a strategic vision statement for your elearning project should provide direction regarding the organizational activities to be pursued and the elearning capabilities your organization plans to develop. It should infuse your organization with a sense of purposeful action. Where do you see your elearning vision three months

from now? How about one year, three to five years, or five to ten years into the future?

Conclusion

Crafting a remarkable vision statement isn't just important; it's essential when launching a new project or taking on any endeavor. With three simple steps—brainstorming, refining & editing, and making it actionable—you can create a clear roadmap for success that outlines how your organization plans to achieve its mission efficiently.

Leadership Questions

1. What do you wish to achieve with your distance learning program project long term?

2. How do you see your vision evolving at various milestones, i.e., three months, six months, one year, and five years?

3. How can you articulate your mental picture of what your program will look like and how it will align with your core values in a simplified vision statement?

Step 5–Review and Analyze Your SWOT

After creating your vision statement, it's time to take a look back over your initial SWOT analysis. You will need to decide what specific steps or actions you need to take to move from dreaming about your future elearning project vision to making it an incredible reality. A great way to do this is to copy the contents of your initial SWOT analysis and respond to each entry in detail to create actionable strategies.

Take Advantage of Your Strengths

Your strengths are valuable assets to your organization. After reviewing the strengths you noted in your initial SWOT analysis, how can you use them in this project to execute your organization's vision? To maximize their potential, prioritize them based on relevance to your organization's distance learning goals. You can address each strength in the order of importance so that it aligns with your overall vision for success.

Think about each strength and why it's a strength. They need to be used, or they offer no advantage. Put them into action. If a strength is listed because it's an area of excellence, think about how to use it to your advantage. This is where you need to expend most of your effort.

Leverage any Opportunities

The opportunities you highlighted during a SWOT analysis are key indicators of what future success could look like for your elearning project if appropriately leveraged. Start by identifying which resources (financial, personnel) will need to be allocated toward taking full advantage of these opportunities before moving forward. This will give you an idea of whether it makes financial sense for your organization to pursue specific opportunities at this time or later down the line when more resources become available.

There are often more opportunities than we could ever take advantage of at any given moment. We should pursue only the best opportunities available to execute our vision. Once you've determined the best opportunities to pursue, write down what specific actions you can take to make each opportunity a reality.

Mitigate or Neutralize Your Weaknesses

Identifying organizational weaknesses is just as important as assessing strengths. Mitigating or neutralizing these weaknesses is essential for long-term success. For example, if an organization receives ongoing complaints from its instructors about insufficient support for new technologies, it will want to identify this issue as a potential weakness. To counteract it, the organization might decide to include additional training for new technologies in its instructor training programs. This would ensure that all staff have the necessary skills to feel comfortable using new technologies, thereby reducing the number of complaints and improving overall team satisfaction.

If you have a weakness you have identified which can affect achieving your vision, you will need to develop a documented strategy to turn it into a powerful force you can control as you move forward. You will want to create an action plan which outlines steps for addressing each weakness identified during a SWOT analysis. When possible, assign tasks to team members with the skill set necessary for effectively tackling specific weaknesses. The best strategy is always to invest most of your time in maximizing your strengths. You can outsource areas that are not your strength to expert contractors who can support fulfilling your distance learning project vision.

Eliminate or Protect Against Potential Threats

Threats to successfully creating your distance learning vision will always exist and should not be ignored. You'll want to focus your team primarily on any threats which have the potential to offer the most immediate and severe impact (Woosley, 2013).

Applying the results of your earlier SWOT analysis and assessing its impact on your distance learning vision will provide you with valuable insight and a list of actionable strategies to guide your elearning project toward your vision.

Conclusion

Taking advantage of your strengths and mitigating or neutralizing any weaknesses after conducting a SWOT analysis comes down to ensuring everyone on your team clearly understands their roles and responsibilities within this process from start to finish. With well-defined action plans in place and adequate resources allocated toward pursuing promising opportunities, your organization can set your elearning project for success.

Leadership Questions

1. What actions does your team need to take to maximize strengths and opportunities while mitigating or neutralizing potential threats and weaknesses as you prepare to execute your distance learning vision?

2. Are there outside organizations, resources, or partnerships you can use to fill any identified gaps in what you need to launch your vision successfully?

Step 6—Goal Setting

In working over the years with many academic and business organizations that have wanted to get their systems and training processes online, I have found they all have one thing in common. They have taken the time to sit down and create a clear blueprint for their organizational goals with regard to establishing a distance education program (their vision), and they have created a strategic plan to reach those goals.

Developing Organizational Goals

Creating and launching your elearning vision is more than simply loading information into an elearning course. You need to plan every step of the process carefully in order to get the best result. One way to do this is to develop your elearning project goals before proceeding to the planning phase of the project. This will help ensure that your team resources and productivity actions are vested in activities that will bring you your desired project outcomes.

Developing organizational goals is essential when launching a new project. Having an effective goal-setting plan can help keep your team focused and on track throughout the entire process, which can lead to better results and outcomes in the long run. As any experienced leader knows, a good strategy is key to success.

Setting High-Value Goals

Focusing on high-value goals is critical to achieving your vision for your distance learning project. A high-value goal is one that will be a game-changer for your organization. It will level up your existing distance learning program or the new virtual world you are launching. This type of goal will produce high returns on the time, attention, energy, and resources you are planning to invest in your elearning vision.

Setting high-value goals will ensure your team does not get lost in the day-to-day busywork of low-value targets, which will produce little to no results toward attaining your overall project vision.

In this part of your strategic plan, you should narrow your focus to set high-value goals and create an action plan for your elearning vision. What specific things does your elearning project need to accomplish? Be specific and outline the principal goals for your project—even if it may take years to realize some of them. In this phase, you should imagine the overall impact of your elearning vision on your organization and stakeholders, as well as any legacy impacts it may create for you.

Setting Milestones

In your strategic plan, it's essential to break your ultimate goal into smaller, realistic, and achievable goals. We can usually divide high-value goals into milestones that mark the beginning or end of significant phases of your project. They may also pertain to an important fixed timeline where we must make a decision or when a deadline will occur. Milestones are still big steps, but they help you think of your goals in terms of what you need to achieve them. By creating a map of milestones for your high-value goals, you can begin to grasp what is necessary to achieve them and what you will need to get there.

SMART Goal Setting

Having a clear and measurable goal in mind gives your team focus and direction and helps them stay on task. By setting tangible objectives, you can also measure progress over time, which can help identify areas that need improvement and where you may be underperforming or overperforming. This level of detail provides invaluable insights into your strategy's effectiveness and potential areas for growth.

Developing organizational goals doesn't have to be complicated. A few simple steps can get you started on the right track. The SMART (specific, measurable, attainable, relevant, and time-based goals) method is one of the most effective tools organizational leaders use to reach their elearning project goals consistently (Tracy, 2015). Narrowing the parameters to clearly and precisely define your high-value goals helps to ensure that your organization's objectives are attainable within a defined time frame. Setting SMART goals eliminates generalizing and guesswork, sets a clear timeline, and makes it easier to track your team's progress while identifying any missed milestones.

S = Specific
M = Measurable
A = Achievable
R = Relevant
T = Time-bound

Begin by documenting your most important high-value project goals. Remember that each goal has a specific purpose, an intended outcome, and a defined timeline. Structure your goals accordingly.

Once you've documented and prioritized your high-value goals, you must also identify your smaller milestone goals and rank them from most important to least important. Some example criteria you might use to rank your goals are:

- a goal's *overall impact* on successfully reaching your vision;

- *precedence* with other goals (is it required to reach one of your other goals);

- *looming deadlines* and timing;

- your available *resources* and *budgets*.

Classify Your Goals

1. **Must-Do Goals** – these goals will get your immediate attention over the next 90 days, even if they may take longer to complete. These goals typically have the most significant and tangible return on investment (ROI), but don't have to be financial in nature.

2. **Should-Do Goals** – these are goals that you should corral in the interim while you focus on your Must-Do goals. Promote them as time or opportunities arise, but always act with intention. Some may never be realized, while others will be first in line for the next quarterly planning cycle (Woosley, 2013).

Goal setting is an essential step for success in achieving your elearning vision. Once you have created your SMART elearning project goals, you will break each one down into the specific, clear tasks, and activities needed to accomplish your goals. It's important to periodically review these goals and make adjustments when necessary.

Conclusion

Having strategic goals in place can go a long way in helping teams stay focused and motivated throughout your distance education and training project. Goals provide clarity and direction while also giving you, as a leader, insight into how your strategies are performing over time. When setting organizational goals, the SMART method is one of the most foolproof ways to get started. Keep your objectives specific and clearly defined to ensure they are attainable within a reasonable time frame. By taking these simple steps, you can set your organization up for success in reaching its elearning project goals consistently.

Leadership Questions

1. What high-value goals are critical to achieving your elearning vision for your organization?

2. What smaller goals and milestones should you reach as you work toward your high-value goals?

3. Are the goals you have identified SMART goals?

4. Have you classified your goals as Must-Do goals or Should-Do goals?

Step 7–Your Action Plan

Now that you have established your most important elearning project goals—those required to accomplish your overall virtual learning world vision—you will create an action plan for reaching each goal. Your action plan will list the specific steps and activities required to develop and implement each goal in your elearning project. An action plan is like a roadmap for success; it will help guide you through the entire process from start to finish.

Creating Clarity

An action plan helps bring clarity to your elearning project. It gives everyone involved in the project, including employees, stakeholders, and leadership, a clear understanding of what needs to be done and when. With an action plan, everyone knows how their individual responsibilities fit into the bigger picture and what they need to do to ensure the project stays on track. Without one, there can be confusion, leading to costly delays or even the abandonment of a project altogether.

Begin by creating and prioritizing the actions required for each goal. There will be more things to do than are possible. Put your energy into the most essential things—every goal will have at least one action (likely more).

Creating Your Task List

The primary advantage of breaking down your goals into tasks is that it creates small, actionable, achievable steps for your team. When creating your task list for each goal, make sure you are clear about what each task entails. If any task is still vague, then break it down even further.

Sometimes when we launch toward a new vision, especially in elearning, which for many will represent uncharted territory, it can seem like a very large and insurmountable mountain. But if team members can focus on looking instead at one task or one small step toward a goal, it will feel a lot more achievable. When we break down goals into tasks, we break down what might seem like the impossible into a sequence of doable steps. There should be no doubt that your team can complete each task, which gives them the confidence to move swiftly toward your organizational elearning goal(s).

What Do We Need?

Once you have completed your task list, you will need to consider what kind of support your team will need to achieve each step. Think of all the practical things, whether it's knowledge or professional help your team will need to complete each task. Start planning in advance to ensure that what you need will be there when you need it. If one team member does not have the tools to complete their task, it may delay your overall progress.

Organizing Resources

An action plan can also help organize the resources required for a project to run smoothly. This includes everything from budgeting for materials needed for completion to allocating human resources and scheduling time frames for key tasks that need to be completed by specific deadlines. All these elements are essential when launching any distance learning project. Having an effective organization system in place can help ensure that nothing slips through the cracks and helps to prevent any unnecessary stress or delays during launch day. Your action plan should clarify what resources you'll need to reach your project goals, create a timeline for the tasks required to achieve each goal and determine what team members you'll need to execute it.

Create a Timeline

It's important to create a timeline for your tasks. A timeline will allow you to see what needs to happen for a task to begin and what tasks can happen alongside each other. Creating a timeline for your tasks will help you see your goals in a more achievable light and help your team be more efficient about how they invest their time.

Making Adjustments

When you first start this process, it's hard to know how long things will take and how much effort will be involved. You will often need to make BIG guesstimates, but you will learn and make adjustments along the way.

An action plan makes this much easier, as it gives you quick access to all relevant information at any given time, from who's responsible for what task, specific dates for task completion, how much money you are allocating toward each activity, etc., so you can implement changes quickly if needed, without unnecessarily disrupting other areas of the process.

Conclusion

Launching a new project is exciting. It's the chance to try something new and potentially gain recognition for your hard work. Having an action plan in place before launching your new virtual learning project is invaluable. It helps create clarity for your team while organizing resources and tasks and providing room to make any necessary adjustments as needed throughout each step of the process.

Leadership Questions

1. What actions do you need to take to reach your project goals?

2. What additional resources and support will you require to accomplish the goals you have identified?

3. What are your timelines for reaching each goal and completing your actionable steps toward your virtual education and training project vision?

Step 8–Measurements for Success

Launching a new distance learning project can be incredibly exciting and rewarding. There is nothing like the feeling of watching your vision come to fruition and seeing it grow into something bigger than you ever imagined. But while the enthusiasm of a new virtual learning project can drive success, it's important to remember the importance of measuring progress toward your organizational goals. Here's why.

Measuring Progress Keeps You Focused on Your Higher Goals

When starting a new project, it's easy to get caught up in the excitement and lose sight of your ultimate goal. It's all too easy to become distracted by the latest trends, shiny new apps, or other smaller distracting details that can pop up along the way. By taking regular measurements, you can stay focused on what matters most—reaching your organization's distance learning objectives.

Measuring Progress Helps You Plan for The Future

By tracking progress, you can create realistic timelines for launching your project and plan for potential bumps along the way. With these measurements, you will also be able to determine how much time and resources need to be allocated for future projects and budget for any associated costs. This information provides valuable insights into how long it takes to complete each step and allows you to adjust accordingly in your planning if needed.

Measuring Progress Gives You the Power to Adjust Your Strategy

As your elearning project unfolds, there may be times when certain aspects don't work as expected, or unforeseen obstacles arise that alter your plans. By regularly measuring progress, you can quickly recognize when changes are necessary and develop strategies which will keep your organizational goals on track. This could mean adjusting existing tactics or introducing new ones to achieve your desired results.

Key Performance Indicators (KPIs)

How will you measure success? How will you measure your progress toward your goals and your elearning vision? Sound strategies for measuring progress must be as objective as possible and built in phases (Harrin, 2017).

One way to measure progress is by using Key Performance Indicators (KPIs). KPIs are measurable values that indicate how well a project is moving toward its goals. They can help you identify areas where improvements are needed and track the success of your elearning project over time.

KPIs are a set of metrics that can be used to gauge the performance of your distance learning project against the predetermined targets or goals you have identified in your strategic plan. KPIs help you understand if your project is meeting its objectives and provide you with valuable data on the progress of your project at any point in time. They also allow you to quickly identify areas where there may be weaknesses or areas for improvement within the project.

What KPIs Should You Track?

You need to decide what kind of Key Progress Indicators (KPIs) you will use to create your elearning project scorecard; these are the measurements and indicators which will let you know if you are reaching your goals or falling behind. Once these have been identified, relevant KPIs can be selected, enabling you to track progress against these goals over time. Some popular examples of KPIs include tracking course completion rates, user engagement, learning outcomes, cost-effectiveness, and customer satisfaction ratings.

If you are redesigning or relaunching an existing virtual world, there are other KPIs you may wish to track besides those required to measure the progress of your project. For example, in managing our distance-learning schools, we found it extremely valuable to compare learner demographic information (i.e., age, location, and any partner institution the learner may attend) with patterns of use in our virtual learning world.

Our collected data noted younger learners in grades 9 and 10 were far more likely not to complete their course activities consistently unless they received formal support from their local school, from a tutoring center, or at home with their parents. They did not always require homework/academic support; however, having access to an individual in the role of a coach seemed to reduce overall course attrition rates in a profound way. The coach helped learners develop a personalized activity completion plan at the beginning of their course and checked in with them every few days or once a week to assist with any obstacles which might hinder their progress.

When working with adult learners, we noted a heightened dissatisfaction with courses if too many group or collaborative evaluation activities were required. Interestingly, adult learners seem to enjoy and take part in group discussions; however, they were less satisfied when too many course evaluations would result from a group effort versus their individual work. They felt group evaluation projects were very demanding on their already heavy life schedules.

This valuable feedback resulted from the qualitative feedback questionnaires learners received during their course experience. We then combined it with quantitative demographic data to provide the above-noted results.

Some KPIs May Change in Various Phases of Your Project

It's also important to note that different types of KPIs should be used for different stages of an elearning project, as each stage has a unique set of expectations and requirements. For example, during the development phase, it may be beneficial to focus on user engagement. At the same time, during implementation, it may make more sense to pay attention to cost-effectiveness or customer satisfaction ratings. Tracking key performance indicators over time can give you valuable insight into potential patterns or trends in usage, which can help inform future decisions about how best to move forward with the project.

What is a Project Scorecard?

A project scorecard is a tool that allows your organization to monitor the progress of your virtual learning projects. The scorecard captures the key performance indicators (KPIs) you are using to measure progress and success at different stages of your project. Tracking your KPIs using a scorecard will allow your organization to gain insights into your team's performance. This allows you to determine if you are meeting your goals or if adjustments need to be made.

Your KPIs are the measures and data collected to monitor your project performance. Your project scorecard is used to display graphic indicators which visually communicate the overall success or failure of any KPI in its efforts to achieve a particular goal.

The Benefits of Using a Project Scorecard

The most important benefit of using a scorecard is its ability to provide real-time visibility into your project's performance. By tracking KPIs such as budget, timeline, resources used, learner satisfaction, etc., you can gain clear insight into your current performance to make informed decisions about future direction and resource allocation. Using a scorecard can help ensure that all stakeholders have access to the same information and work toward a common goal. This reduces miscommunication and helps keep everyone on the same page.

Steps to Creating a Project Scorecard:

1. **Define What to Track** – there are a variety of qualitative and quantitative metrics that you can use to track your project progress, for example, achievements against pre-defined development milestones, learner satisfaction (via a metric such as surveys), team satisfaction, and budget figures such as running costs.

2. **Set Targets** – Once you have defined which measures you will use, you must decide what constitutes a positive or quality result in your measures. For example, achieving 80% learner satisfaction with a new course's look, feel, and functioning may be

considered a positive result. However, if you are on track to reach 80% of revenue goals after launching your new project, this may not represent a quality result for your organization. Work with your team to decide the acceptable targets for each measure and then establish how you will incorporate these into your scorecard.

3. **Populate the Measures** – you'll need to decide which team members will be responsible for gathering data and populating the information you require for your scorecard. This will give you a snapshot of your project progress. You'll also need to define the frequency for populating fresh scorecard data (i.e., ongoing, weekly, monthly, etc.).

4. **Communicate the Results** – how will you communicate the results to your team? Some examples other organizations use include weekly team huddles/meetings, the circulation of reports, or an automated online metrics reporting page.

5. **Evaluate Scorecard Results** – once results have been communicated, you'll need to meet with your team to review them. You can then decide if any modifications or adjustments are required to your original strategic plan as you proceed toward your elearning goal.

Using a scorecard will help your organization create objective measures of your strategic plan progress and ensure you meet your elearning project objectives. This also ensures that your project and its initiatives tightly focus on delivering the most strategic objectives within your prescribed timelines and allotted resources.

Conclusion

Taking regular measurements toward your organizational goals helps keep you focused on what matters, allows you to plan for future virtual learning projects more effectively, and gives you the power to adjust your strategy if needed to reach your objectives successfully. KPIs are an excellent way for your organization to measure your progress in your elearning project. They provide valuable data on whether objectives are being met and help identify areas where improvements may need to be made in your project. Organizations use an elearning project scorecard as a powerful tool to provide real-time visibility into KPI performance metrics. This can offer you invaluable insight into where your elearning project stands so you can make informed decisions about how best to move forward.

Leadership Questions

1. What are the most critical indicators of success as your team works toward achieving your elearning project vision and goals?

2. Which KPIs will you use as measurements and indicators to track the progress and success of your distance learning project?

3. How will you gather and analyze, and then communicate the results of your KPI data into a project scorecard for your team?

# 7

FUTURE EDUCATION VIRTUAL CLASSROOMS AND BEYOND

… ELEARNING GOLD—ANNETTE LEVESQUE

The Future of Virtual Learning: What It Looks Like and Why We Need It

The pandemic event of 2020 has forced us to rethink how we teach and learn. From online classes to remote exams, providing learners with flexible education options that include virtual education and training has become a necessity rather than a choice. The new availability of digital learning has opened up an entire world of possibilities for educators and learners alike. But what predictions for the future can we make?

Increased Hybrid Learning Models

The future of distance learning is likely a combination of online and in-person learning. Hybrid learning allows students and teachers to reap the benefits of both worlds. With online classes, students have access to lectures, assignments, and resources anytime, anywhere. On the other hand, in-person classes provide students with valuable social interactions and hands-on experiences. A hybrid approach can help mitigate some of the negative effects of distance learning, such as isolation and lack of participation.

Greater Personalization

Digital learning platforms have made it easier than ever to personalize education. In the future, personalized virtual learning will become even more prevalent. Students will be able to learn at their own pace, receive individual feedback, and have custom-tailored assignments. Personalized learning will enable learners to take ownership of their education and learn in a way that suits their needs.

Increased Availability of Virtual Reality

Virtual Reality (VR) provides an immersive learning experience that can transport learners to distant lands, historical events, and scientific phenomena. VR can help students visualize abstract concepts, experience simulations, and explore new environments. It has the potential to revolutionize distance learning by creating learning environments that are difficult or impossible to create in real life.

Lifelong Learning

The future of distance learning is focused on lifelong learning. As technology continues to evolve and the job market changes, workers will need to acquire new skills and knowledge. Distance learning provides the flexibility and accessibility to help workers learn new skills or take up new hobbies. Learning is no longer just about education but also about self-improvement and personal development.

ELEARNING GOLD—ANNETTE LEVESQUE

Artificial Intelligence (AI) Revolutionizing Education

Artificial intelligence (AI) is a technology that has been gaining momentum in our world for many years. At its most basic level, artificial intelligence (AI) is a type of technology that enables machines to simulate human behavior. This means that AI-enabled machines can take on tasks such as decision-making, problem-solving, and even language processing to complete tasks autonomously. AI is often combined with other technologies, such as machine learning, deep learning, natural language processing, and computer vision, to enable machines to "learn" over time and more efficiently complete specific tasks.

The Emergence of AI Chatbots

AI Chatbots, such as ChatGPT, are changing the educational landscape and offering a new interactive medium for learners to untangle complex concepts. This advanced, intuitive chatbot launched by OpenAI on November 30, 2022, swiftly caught the attention of a million users within its first five days. Claiming human-like efficiency, ChatGPT can genuinely explain, program, and argue.

In order for an AI program to operate effectively, it relies on algorithms, which are sets of instructions that guide the machine's data processing and decision-making. These algorithms enable the AI system to analyze and interpret our user input data. AI models such as ChatGPT are typically trained on large datasets to learn patterns and correlations. It's important to note that the model's responses are generated based on statistical patterns learned from the training data rather than genuine comprehension or reasoning. The machine may also use additional information, such as past experiences or external sources, to refine its decision-making process over time. AI's contextual learning component allows machines like ChatGPT to become increasingly accurate at completing tasks without needing additional human input.

How Can We Use Future AI Tools to Benefit Education?

Artificial Intelligence (AI) is revolutionizing almost every aspect of our lives, and the education sector is no exception. AI has the potential to transform traditional teaching methods, improve student engagement, and make learning more accessible than ever before. Other future benefits to education include:

1. Personalization and Customization

AI-enabled systems can tailor instruction to individual learner needs and preferences, fostering an adaptive learning environment. Adaptive learning platforms leverage machine algorithms to create personalized, interactive learning experiences that adjust based on a student's performance levels.

We can use these platforms in physical classrooms and online learning environments to personalize instruction and allow students to progress at their own pace. Adaptive learning platforms offer valuable feedback on each student's progress, allowing teachers to better understand their students' strengths and weaknesses to tailor instruction accordingly.

2. Increased Accessibility and Inclusivity

Ensuring equitable access to education and training is vital. AI-based tools, such as language translation and voice-to-text systems, can overcome barriers faced by students with disabilities, non-native speakers, and historically marginalized populations.

3. Teacher-Student Relationship Dynamics

Using AI in education will significantly affect the roles of teachers and students. Nobody wants to learn with an autobot. You will want to consider how AI can complement human instruction within your organization rather than replace it.

4. Continuous Professional Development

The integration of AI necessitates continuous skill development and technology training for both instructors and administrators. Organizations must provide opportunities for ongoing education in AI technology to ensure that staff members can effectively use, manage, and evaluate AI-driven tools and programs.

New Challenges Presented by AI

Despite its potential benefits, there are also potential drawbacks associated with using AI in the classroom. One of the primary concerns is that these technologies could lead to an imbalance between instructor-led learning and computer-led instruction. Too much emphasis on automated systems reduces the importance of face-to-face interaction between instructors and learners, an essential component in creating meaningful learning experiences. Another potential issue is that AI technologies can only go so far when it comes to understanding human behavior. They may not always be able to accurately interpret complex social situations or subtle cues that are a part of human interaction and connection.

Other potential challenges for leaders and their distance learning teams to consider include the following:

Search Engines vs. AI
AI is predicted to replace search engines in the future. However, unlike search engines, there are occurrences where AI makes stuff up when it doesn't have an answer to a query. Google's new AI Chatbot Bard was announced in Feb 2023 as a rival to the popular ChatGPT launched by OpenAI. But the bot confidently made a factual error in its very first demo.

The systems frequently offer fictionalized information because they are essentially autocomplete systems. Rather than querying a database of proven facts to answer questions, they are trained on vast amounts of text and analyze patterns to determine which word follows the next in any given sentence (Vincent, 2023).

The tendency of AI chatbots to confidently present incorrect information as fact to its users may present new challenges requiring learners to develop new skill sets regarding research and validating the information they are receiving from their queries. Additionally, there needs to be more concern about companies that own AI Chatbots having total control over the information and results presented to users. Often a single result is generated by an AI Chatbot vs. a page of indexed results users can validate when using a search engine. And currently, no cited sources are included in an AI result. Instructors will need to emphasize exploring strategies for teaching learners how to identify potential biases and errors in AI-generated information, fact-check claims, and determine when it is more appropriate to seek information from other sources.

Fears of Increased Plagiarism
AI Chatbots can be helpful to instructors and students in ways such as providing prompts to get past the fear of the blank page and aiding with the analysis of large amounts of data. But amidst this incredible potential lies the looming risk of increasing plagiarism. There is too little data yet to assess the threat from bots like ChatGPT; they could negatively impact academic standards if learners depend on them instead of creating original works.

As technology advances, university leaders and instructors are also feeling pressure to keep up with learners who can sometimes learn about AI advancements faster than their professors through social media. It is unknown whether plagiarism detection systems currently used by universities, and colleges will be able to keep pace with the rapid innovations of newer open AI technologies now available to learners.

New Evaluation Practices Required
While grading AI-generated texts could become standard practice in the future, editing and correcting these texts would still require real knowledge of a subject. Thus, one strategy for organizations offering virtual education and training programs may be to supplement current learner evaluation practices with supplementary oral discussions about the work submitted. If a learner can submit an A+ essay, they should also be able to discuss and elaborate on the ideas in their submission.

Ethical Considerations
As instructors and students embrace AI as a tool for learning, it is important to consider the ethical implications of its use in the classroom. Technology should be used to enhance educational experiences while upholding ethical standards and protecting the rights of learners. AI in education raises many ethical concerns, such as the potential for biased algorithms in student assessment and the invasion of privacy because of data collection mechanisms.

Data Privacy

Data privacy is one of the biggest ethical concerns with using AI in the classroom. AI relies heavily on vast amounts of data, raising concerns about privacy and security. With more learner information available to organizations, it is essential to consider how this data will be used and protected. Instructors should ensure they are transparent about what kinds of data they are collecting from their students and how it will be used and stored (especially if they are working remotely from home computers). Any data collected should only be used for educational purposes and not shared with third parties without consent. Leaders must address these concerns by setting policies on data collection, storage, and sharing while implementing robust cybersecurity measures to protect sensitive information.

Fairness and Bias

Another primary ethical concern when using AI in education is fairness and bias. For example, some algorithms have been found to have a greater error rate for certain marginalized groups than others due to built-in biases or skewed training data sets.

To prevent such bias from influencing student outcomes, organizational leaders must take steps to ensure that any algorithms in the technological tools they are using are free from bias and accurately reflect real-world results. This is an important conversation to have with vendors of technology tools before acquiring them for your education and training program.

You can also conduct identity-masked testing within your organization and provide an independent oversight committee. These strategies will help ensure that any technologies used in your virtual program employ fair and equitable algorithms for all learners.

By being mindful of these considerations, such as data privacy, fairness, and bias, educators can create an inclusive environment where all students can learn equally, no matter their backgrounds or abilities, while still leveraging the power of AI to enhance their learning experience.

Conclusion

As education rapidly evolves, distance learning has emerged as a key driver in unlocking its full potential. From personalized learning to virtual reality, education is poised for a revolution. One of the most exciting developments is the integration of artificial intelligence. While it offers many benefits, it's crucial to consider the ethical implications for instructors and learners alike. Organizational leaders must take steps to ensure that the rights of all individuals are protected. By embracing virtual learning, organizations can offer outstanding distance education programs while helping learners remain competitive in an ever-changing world and job market. It's an exciting time to be part of the education landscape, and we're just getting started.

Leadership Questions

1. What impact has new innovations in education and technology had on your organization?

2. How can AI Chatbots be integrated into your distance education and training program to enhance learner engagement?

3. How can you prepare your learners to critically evaluate the accuracy and reliability of AI-generated information?

4. How can you overcome some of the potential ethical dilemmas associated with using AI in your elearning programs?

5. In what ways do you see your distance education and training program evolving to meet the needs of your future learners?

REFERENCES

AL-Hunaiyyan, A., Al-Huwail, N., & Al-Sharhan, S. (2008). Blended e-learning design: Discussion of cultural issues. *International Journal of Cyber Society and Education, 1*(1), 17–32. Retrieved February 27, 2021, from https://core.ac.uk/download/pdf/25712517.pdf.

Anderson, T. (2011). *The theory and practice of online learning, second edition.* Athabasca University Press. Retrieved from http://www.aupress.ca/index.php/books/120146

BDC. (2020, September 12). *SWOT analysis: An easy tool for strategic planning.* BDC.ca. Retrieved January 19, 2021, from https://www.bdc.ca/en/articles-tools/business-strategy-planning/define-strategy/swot-analysis-easy-tool-strategic-planning?

BigCommerce. (2021, January 17). *ECommerce and Marketing Strategy: How to write a powerful mission statement that resonates.* BigCommerce. Retrieved January 20, 2021, from https://www.bigcommerce.com/ecommerce-answers/how-to-write-a-powerful-effective-mission-statement/

Bressler, L. A., Bressler, M. S., & Bressler, M. E. (2011). Demographic and psychographic variables and the effect on online student success. *Journal of Technology Research.* Retrieved from https://www.researchgate.net/publication/242465497_Demographic_and_psychographic_variables_and_the_effect_on_online_student_success.

Canonico, M. (2020, November 23). *What is learner autonomy?* Docebo. Retrieved February 16, 2021, from https://www.docebo.com/blog/what-is-learner-autonomy/

Ellis, S. (2020, July 13). *What is mastery learning?* Getting Smart. Retrieved February 15, 2021, from https://www.gettingsmart.com/2019/08/what-is-mastery-learning/

Fisher, D., Frey, N., & Hattie, J. (2021). *The distance learning playbook Grades K-12: Teaching for engagement & impact in any setting.* Corwin Press, Inc., a Sage Publishing Company.

GSA. (2020, July). *IT accessibility laws and policies.* IT Accessibility Laws and Policies | Section508.gov. Retrieved March 16, 2021, from https://www.section508.gov/manage/laws-and-policies

Gutierrez, K. (n.d.). *Elearning interactivity: When it works and when it goes wrong.* SHIFT. Retrieved May 22, 2022, from https://www.shiftelearning.com/blog/bid/312814/elearning-interactivity-when-it-works-and-when-it-goes-wrong

Harrin, E. (2017, January 19). *How to build a project scorecard.* Project Management.com. Retrieved January 26, 2021, from https://www.projectmanagement.com/blog-post/26027/How-To-Build-A-Project-Scorecard

Harvard University. (2015, September 8). *Learning communities.* Center on the Developing Child at Harvard University. Retrieved May 22, 2022, from https://developingchild.harvard.edu/collective-change/key-concepts/learning-communities/

Hutchinson, M., Tin, T., & Cao, Y. (2008). *"In-your-pocket" and "On-the-fly:" Meeting the needs of today's new generation of online learners with mobile learning technology.* AU press-Digital Publications. Retrieved April 3, 2022, from https://read.

References

aupress.ca/read/the-theory-and-practice-of-online-learning/section/94680e32-069e-40b6-90eb-225ad10076d5

International Telecommunication Union. (2021). *Mobile network coverage*. International Telecommunication Union. Retrieved October 3, 2022, from https://www.itu.int/itu-d/reports/statistics/2021/11/15/mobile-network-coverage/

Kolloff, M. A. (2011). *Strategies for effective student/student interaction in online courses*. studylib.net. Retrieved April 3, 2021, from https://studylib.net/doc/18404369/strategies-for-effective-student-student-interaction-in-o...

Linney, S. (2020, November 12). *Reimagining education after COVID-19*. QS. Retrieved March 14, 2021, from https://www.qs.com/reimagining-education-after-covid-19/

Moore, M. G. (1989). Editorial: Three types of interaction. *American Journal of Distance Education*, *3*(2), 1–7. https://doi.org/10.1080/08923648909526659

Morris, S., Fawcett, G., Brisebois, L., & Hughes, J. (2018, November 28). *A demographic, employment, and income profile of Canadians with disabilities aged 15 years and over, 2017*. Statistics Canada: Canadian Survey on Disability Reports. Retrieved March 14, 2021, from https://www150.statcan.gc.ca/n1/pub/89-654-x/89-654-x2018002-eng.htm

OnStrategy. (2019, April 30). *How to develop strategy mission, vision & values*. OnStrategy - Developing Strategy. Retrieved January 20, 2021, from https://onstrategyhq.com/resources/developing-your-strategy/

Pappas, C. (2018, March 9). *7 tips to determine your eLearning project goals*. eLearning Industry. Retrieved January 16, 2021, from https://elearningindustry.com/tips-determine-elearning-project-goals

Parsons, N. (2019, September 12). *What is a SWOT analysis, and how to do it right (with examples)*. LivePlan Blog. Retrieved January 18, 2021, from https://www.liveplan.com/blog/what-is-a-swot-analysis-and-how-to-do-it-right-with-examples/

Pritts, N. (2020, December 7). *Using announcements to give narrative shape to your online course: Faculty focus*. Faculty Focus | Higher Ed Teaching & Learning. Retrieved March 2, 2021, from https://www.facultyfocus.com/articles/online-education/online-course-design-and-preparation/using-announcements-to-give-narrative-shape-to-your-online-course/

Shale, D., & Garrison, D. R. (1990). *Education at a distance: From issues to practice.*

Sinek, S. (2019). *Start with why: How great leaders inspire everyone to take action*. Penguin Business.

Siteimprove. (2021). *Include everyone, keep everyone: Your guide to web accessibility in Canada*. Siteimprove. Retrieved March 14, 2021, from https://siteimprove.com/en-ca/accessibility/2020-guide-web-accessibility-canada/.

Taylor, A. (2016, July 5). *Why are values important for strategic planning?* Strategic planning facilitator Vancouver. Retrieved January 20, 2021, from https://www.smestrategy.net/blog/why-are-values-important-for-strategic-planning

TBS. (2021, February 18). *Synchronous learning vs. asynchronous learning in online education*. TheBestSchools.org. Retrieved March 7, 2021, from https://thebestschools.org/magazine/synchronous-vs-asynchronous-education/

References

Thomson, G. (2018, October 24). *What is the information and communications standards?* Accessibility for Ontarians with Disabilities Act (AODA). Retrieved March 15, 2021, from https://aoda.ca/what-is-the-information-and-communications-standards/

Tracy, B. (2015, May 12). *Setting your goals.* Brian Tracy's Self Improvement & Professional Development Blog. Retrieved January 12, 2021, from https://www.briantracy.com/blog/personal-success/setting-your-goals/

U.S. Department of Justice Civil Rights Division. (2020, February 28). *What is the Americans with Disabilities Act (ADA)?* ADA.gov. Retrieved March 30, 2023, from https://www.ada.gov/resources/disability-rights-guide/

Vaughan, N. D., Cleveland-Innes, M., & Garrison, D. R. (2013). *Teaching in blended learning environments: Creating and sustaining communities of inquiry.* AU Press.

Vincent, J. (2023, February 8). *Google's AI chatbot bard makes factual error in first demo.* The Verge. Retrieved March 18, 2023, from https://www.theverge.com/2023/2/8/23590864/google-ai-chatbot-bard-mistake-error-exoplanet-demo

W3C Web Accessibility Initiative. (2023, January 25). *Web content accessibility guidelines (WCAG) 2.2.* W3C. Retrieved March 28, 2023, from https://www.w3.org/WAI/standards-guidelines/

Wagner, E. D. (1994). In support of a functional definition of interaction. *American Journal of Distance Education, 8*(2), 6–29. https://doi.org/10.1080/08923649409526852

Woosley, J. (2013). *Conquer the entrepreneur's kryptonite.* Free Agent Press.

NEED MORE HELP WITH YOUR DISTANCE LEARNING PROGRAM?

Annette is a highly proficient consultant and coach in the academic and corporate sectors, with a wealth of knowledge and experience in virtual education and training. She also has in-depth expertise in the latest trends and advancements in this constantly evolving field. She can help your organization build and execute a strategic plan to deliver the highest quality distance education and training solutions.

Readers of this book can sign up for free resources at:
www.AnnetteLevesque.com/readers

Made in the USA
Monee, IL
28 April 2026

49136197R00174